Surviving the Sermon

Surviving the Sermon

A Guide to Preaching for Those Who Have to Listen

David J. Schlafer

COWLEY PUBLICATIONS
Cambridge ✦ Boston
Massachusetts

Published in the United States of America by Cowley Publications, a division of the Society of St. John the Evangelist. No portion of this book may be reproduced, stored in or introduced into a retrieval system, or transmitted, in any form or by any means—including photocopying—without the prior written permission of Cowley Publications, except in the case of brief quotations embodied in critical articles and reviews.

International Standard Book Number: 1-56101-064-2

Library of Congress Number: 92-19363

Library of Congress Cataloging-in-Publication Data

Schlafer, David J., 1944 -

Surviving the sermon : a guide to preaching for those who have to listen / David J. Schlafer.

p. cm.

ISBN 1-56101-064-2 (alk. paper).

1. Preaching 2. Listening—Religious aspects—Christianity. 3. Christian life—1960-

I. Title.

BV4235.L57S35 1992

251—dc20   92-10806

Cover illustrations from William Hogarth's engraving, *The Sleeping Congregation*

This book is printed on acid-free paper and was produced in the United States of America.

Third Printing

Cowley Publications
28 Temple Place
Boston, Massachusetts 02111

For Linda,
Kirk, and Kristen
who listen deeply,
speak clearly,
and dance the Gospel gracefully.

Acknowledgments

I am deeply grateful ...

to the dean, faculty, students, and staff at the School of Theology, University of the South, for their support as this book was written during my year in residence as visiting professor, especially to Christopher Bryan for his valuable suggestions;

to my colleagues in the Academy of Homiletics, especially O. C. Edwards, Eugene Lowry, Charles Rice, and Thomas Troeger;

to my editor, Cynthia Shattuck, who first suggested the book and shepherded it skillfully to completion, and to Vicki Black, who served as copy-editor;

to Chester A. LaRue and Jay Rochelle for permission to use their sermons in this book;

and to the members of my family,
—Linda, who supported my vocation to write long before I knew of it myself,
—Kirk, who patiently pulled me through the inscrutabilities of computerese and cheered me along,
—Kristen, who talked me through the opening chapters, worked with me on the final version, and years ago provided the finest illustration I know of how preaching works.

David J. Schlafer

Table of Contents

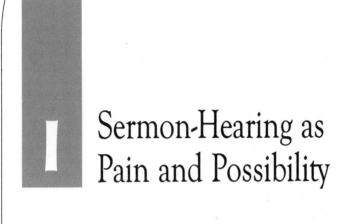

Sermon-Hearing as Pain and Possibility

1

Hunger Without Appetite

The sermon was dragging on—longer and longer. The preacher was droning on—duller and duller. From a far corner of the church came the clear, plaintive question of a five year old: "Mommy, can we please just pay the man and go home?"

Two figures face each other stiffly in a recent cartoon. One is obviously a cleric; the other obviously is not. The layman says to the minister: "Your sermon was kind of preachy."

The preacher stands before the congregation and begins: "My sermon today is on the problem of evil. Can any of you think of bad things that happen to good people?" In chorus the congregation responds: "Your sermons."

STORIES ABOUT BAD PREACHING make good jokes—or frequent jokes, anyway. When sermons strike us as insipid, insufferable, or just plain boring, comic relief can be a good way to vent our frustrations. But sermon humor often masks a sense of tragedy.

"Dr. Gillespie, I am almost in despair," said a women to the president of Princeton Theological Seminary not long ago. She was in her mid-fifties, serving on the pulpit committee of a large church that was searching for a new pastor. Having listened to sermons from a number of prospective candidates, the woman was on the edge of losing her patience. "Every Sunday I psych myself up for a positive experience," she complained, "and then I come out of that church asking myself: 'Is this what preaching has come to?'"

"My experience," President Gillespie later observed, "is that the woman's name is legion, for she speaks for many." Exactly how many, of course, no one can say. But the woman is surely not alone. I know an executive in New York's financial district who carries a copy of the Sunday newspaper into the church pew. That way, he figures, the interval between the gospel lesson and the creed will not be simply dead time.

Why do cartoons of preachers and humorous anecdotes about preaching strike such responsive chords? Why do horror stories about preaching evoke so much sympathy and so little surprise? It would be one thing if such tales could be passed off as ignorance or deliberate misrepresentation from those outside the Christian community. But much sermon humor consists of inside jokes, and much of the frustration it thinly veils suggests deep hunger on the part of listeners. Hunger, and perhaps hope for something better in spite of experience to the contrary. For why, after all, would people continue to criticize what they really do not care about?

Those who give sermons often find preaching as hard to engage as those who have to listen. An advertisement for a homily service that distributes canned sermons makes this revealing sales pitch: "You'll never again be working late Saturday night, getting your homily ready. You'll never again have to scour other resources, looking for an inspiring base."

What a strange way to sell sermons! What a strange understanding of what sermons are and what they are supposed to do! It is as though a frozen fast food company were offering professional chefs in gourmet restaurants the chance to renounce any investment in fine cooking. How could anyone who cared about cooking or about eating have the slightest interest in such an offer? Yet this homily service, as it proudly proclaims, is doing a thriving business. It reprints glowing testimonials of satisfied customers, and even offers a money-back guarantee.

Managing a good restaurant is surely a complex and demanding enterprise. But how odd it would be if, in the midst of making sure that dishes got washed and books got balanced, the supervising chef could not find the time or the joy for cooking and sharing food. It is to just such a problem, however, that this homily service addresses itself with unblushing candor: "These days we know you spend as much time as an administrator as you do in spiritual leadership," it commiserates. "We can give you back ten hours a week. You can use these sermons just as they come to you, or you can insert your own thoughts and local references." In either case, "You'll never again have to 'wing it' without properly prepared notes because some emergency ate up the precious time you had set aside for the preparation of a homily."

Then comes the clinching argument: "Think for a moment: couldn't you put to better, more profitable use those hours you now spend writing a weekly homily that once spoken becomes only a reminder that you have to write another next week?"

Is this what preaching has come to?

There are doubtless many factors that contribute to the unsatisfied hunger and lack of appetite felt simultaneously on both sides of the pulpit. Ever-increasing demands on a pastor's life do compete for the time it takes to prepare for preaching. The administrative, physical, and pastoral responsibilities of a parish minister can be overwhelming. Many churches cannot afford adequate professional staffing. Counseling, programs in social ministry, evangelistic outreach—there are always more than enough worthy candidates waiting at the door of the preacher's study to consume all of the time and energy available. Yet, when in the history of the church has it ever been any different?

Maybe preaching sometimes fails to satisfy because preachers are poorly equipped to undertake their task: they may not be too busy to preach well, they may just not know how! The suggestion is plausible. There has been a sharp increase in "late vocation" candidates for ordained ministry over the last several years. Competent in the particular skills and techniques of their first careers, many of these candidates nevertheless lack much education in literature, rhetoric, philosophy, history, or the arts—all of which are important resources for good preaching. Yet, again, some of the most powerful preachers in the life of the church have been "unlearned, ignorant men" (and women), as the book of Acts puts it. (And one suspects that some of the best educated preachers have also been among the most deadly!) Clergy education is an important thing, but it is not the only thing.

Perhaps responsibility for dissatisfaction with preaching lies as much with those who sit in the pew as it does with those who mount the pulpit. Many listeners are as poorly prepared to hear sermons as many preachers are to preach them. The effects of a "Sesame Street," sound-byte video culture are pervasive. Attention spans are short; critical reasoning skills are limited. The level of biblical and ecclesiastical literacy is decreasing among those to whom preaching is addressed. Older church members may have been raised on Bible stories, rigorous confirmation classes, and a regular rhythm of church-related activities; the learning environments of many younger members are both less regimented, and less graced.

Yes, but (the question comes again) must we presuppose either a high level of literacy or a firm grounding in Christian tradition as an essential condition for effective preaching? If so, the message of the Gospel would never have gotten off the ground in the first place. Maybe faltering literacy and rising secularity in culture are not the problem. Maybe the problem with preaching is a problem with authority. Claims to authority come from every conceivable quarter. Public opinion is constantly and subtly swayed by advertisers and political analysts, yet most people are jaded by, and highly resistant to, any directly asserted authoritative claim. "Where do you get off," they bristle, "trying to *preach* to me like that!" There was a time when the preacher's voice carried considerable weight in the pulpit and the community. Such authority is seldom granted automatically anymore. Still, Christian proclamation has always had to set forth its case among other competing claims, and resistance to authority is hardly a late-breaking cultural phenomenon.

In a word, it is not hard to imagine a number of things that might contribute to a depressed appetite but an increased hunger for preaching. Yet effective preaching has always been possible in the midst of conditions that make it difficult. Furthermore, the church is commanded to preach the Gospel no matter how difficult the conditions may be. It is the promise of God that such proclamations will not return empty, but will prosper and accomplish their intended work. The question before us is as simple, and as profound, as this: how can that which we preach and hear quicken our appetites and nourish our hunger? While we need to be alert and responsive to conditioning factors, finding scapegoats or making excuses is ultimately beside the point.

Preaching has received a great deal of attention in recent years. "Good preacher" often ranks at the top of qualifications desired in a candidate to serve a congregation as pastor or priest. A great deal of work has been done in the last ten to fifteen years by those who teach and write about preaching. In seminary courses, continuing education seminars, books, and articles, preachers are being encouraged to shape sermons that are more accessible to the contours of the contemporary mindset and more faithful to the spirit of biblical material. Eventually the effects of this "new homiletic" may filter down to congregations. Perhaps negative perceptions of preaching may change in time.

Yet it would be naive to think that appetite for and confidence in preaching can be achieved simply by introducing and mastering new techniques for sermon preparation and delivery. Indeed, focusing exclusively on such techniques tends to treat sermon listeners as though they were passive and manipulable, as though they were simply buying a bill of goods. If congregations were merely consumer markets, perhaps they could be surveyed and managed. Some church organizations seem to operate as though this were the case. Yet the proclamation of the Gospel is not the same as the promotion of a product. The good news of Jesus Christ celebrates and invites relationship with a Person; it is not amenable to any conceivable "spin" in order to make it palatable to every taste. God's self-disclosing invitation to fellowship comes on its own terms. Preachers have a truth to announce, not an option to peddle. The Gospel does not coerce or "hook" those it addresses, and preaching must respect human dignity even as it asserts our fundamental dependence upon God.

Sermons are preached and heard in a context that is shot through with a consumer mind-set, however. It is not surprising, therefore, that criticism of sermons often has the flavor of conflicting and shifting consumer sentiment. What constitutes "good" preaching seems to depend upon the ear of the listener. For some, a good sermon is one that blesses and reinforces the economic and political status quo; for others, it is one that subverts and shakes up "the system." Everyone agrees that a sermon should be relevant to life, but relevance seems to involve "different strokes for different folks." Many sermon listeners indicate that they want preaching to be biblical. For some, however, this will consist in liberally quoting and cross-referencing Scripture passages, or in verse-by-verse exegesis. For others, it means a recounting of Bible stories, or a systematic treatment of biblical themes. Still others are convinced that biblical preaching is exhortation to embrace and uphold certain precepts of personal morality, or particular codes of behavior.

Perhaps it is no wonder that preachers sometimes feel beaten before they start. Opinions as to what makes for good preaching differ within denominations, within local churches, and even among individuals. It is discouraging to feel that one will always be weighed and found wanting on somebody's scale—and sometimes on conflicting scales simultaneously. Judgments pronounced on preaching are often strong without being clear—either to the preacher or to those who judge—but such judgments have significant impact on the preacher's job security and on prospects for professional advancement as well.

When consumers get fed up with products in the market-place, they can resort to consumer advocacy. Disaffection with preaching is seldom organized with analogous sophistication. By and large, one by one, disgruntled parishioners vote with their feet and with their checkbooks. Rarely does this disillu-sionment give rise to concerted action; if so, it does not extend beyond giving the local pastor the boot. This is probably a mercy—although preachers perhaps should not be too compla-cent about this situation!

Preachers and those who listen to them are bound together far more intimately than are those who play the roles of pur-veyor and consumer in the dramas of economics. To publish a manifesto of the rights of sermon-hearers would not be very constructive, yet a word does need to be said, not just on behalf of, but explicitly directed to, those who listen to sermons week after week. These listeners are entitled to an inside view of what happens in the making of a sermon, and how it is that a ser-mon effectively does its job. The privilege of preaching is usu-ally reserved for those who are licensed by their denominations after extensive theological training, but the preaching process is not an esoteric enterprise.

Those who listen to preaching deserve, and are even respon-sible for, some understanding of what they should be hearing and what they can be listening for. It is essential for all who share in the ministry of the Word to have a clear and mutual understanding as to how that ministry unfolds.

The feeling, however, that preaching is the exclusive prov-ince of the ordained can be difficult to dislodge. Apart from hesitating to tell preachers their business, many sermon listen-ers are reluctant to approach preaching analytically. Will not the effectiveness of the sermon in the life of the listener be un-dermined by approaching it with a technical ear? Would one really deal effectively with a listless appetite by developing the skills of a food critic? Preaching is for spiritual nourishment. How can we receive the word of God for us if we are listening for outlines, scriptural scholarship, theology, and apt illustrations?

These are valid questions. Most of us have probably encountered sermon listeners who are as fussy as gourmet restaurant critics. Any sermon they hear is an occasion for the wielding of a dissecting scalpel. While they could be savoring and digesting what the preacher has offered, instead they are conducting a coldly dispassionate postmortem on it, and cutting the preacher to ribbons in the process. Yet the potential drawbacks of these analytical skills should not inhibit us from employing them appropriately.

Our appreciation for a play, a dance, a symphony, a poem, or an athletic event can be enriched by some understanding of the dynamics of the medium. Yes, it takes a while to get the feel of what to look or listen for. There can be periods of awkwardness, and it may even seem for a time that we have lost something very precious. After all, we felt a warm inspiration when our senses were "washed over" by the beauty of dance costumes, the excitement of players scoring, or the rich sweeping sounds of a full orchestra. Now that is gone, as we struggle to track with many different sights and sounds all at once. Nothing seems to fit together.

But if we stick with it, eventually we begin to participate in a far deeper way, whereas before we were only observers. And when the performance is over, we have more than a vague and fading memory of satisfaction. We have at our disposal a vast treasure for extended reflection and fresh insight.

Preaching is meant to engage us as participants in ways that are far more radical than any literary, musical, athletic, or artistic event. Many people speak of being profoundly moved by their experiences of art, drama, music, or sport; such encounters can, in fact, be life changing. Christians believe that through the hearing of Gospel preaching, we can be moved at the deepest level of our being—moved toward freedom from enslaving habits, terrifying illusions, and destructive hatreds; moved toward understanding of God and of ourselves; moved toward action that helps to break the chains and heal the wounds of others. Of course the grace of God can transform those who have never thought for a moment about the preaching process, but God invites and desires our progressively deeper participation in the drama of redemption through the grace of Christ.

Those who listen to preaching can learn to engage it, and the transforming power that comes through it, more actively and intimately as they come to understand it more reflectively and analytically. Helping those who listen to participate more fully in preaching is the purpose of this book. Sermons need not be endurance exercises simply to be survived; they can be experiences through which God's resurrecting life takes actual shape and direction for those who listen. Sermons can become sources of spiritual survival.

All your frustrations with preaching will not necessarily dissipate if you come to understand and participate in preaching more fully. You may find yourself stuck with poor preaching, and need to take some action: to confront your preacher constructively, to search elsewhere for the spiritual nourishment that comes through preaching, to begin shaping your own sermons as a spiritual exercise, to wrestle with a preaching vocation, or even to make the kind of jokes about preaching that can be occasions of grace, rather than simply expressions of despair.

It is quite possible, however, that even if your frustrations with preaching do not abate, they may begin to take a different form. You may find that what you used to like about sermons does not satisfy nearly so well, and that what used to irritate you, while still painful, is a productive pain. You may find occasions for further insight as you talk with others—not about whether they "liked" the sermon, but about how the word of God distinctively encountered them in what they heard. You may discover that you have the ability to interact with the material of the sermon in such a way that, even if the preacher is preaching badly, you can still find resources for spiritual growth.

One result of reading this book may be a deeper comprehension and a more firmly grounded appreciation of what you already value in sermons. Some of us, after all, have been blessed by hearing good preaching, maybe even by hearing different styles of good preaching. We may know more about preaching than we can articulate, and need help only in learning how to express that understanding in ways that will be useful.

Ideally, a deeper understanding of the sermon process may have other benefits as well. You may be in a better position to offer your talents in a search process when the time comes for your church to call a new pastor—one who knows how to preach well. Whether your preacher is "excellent," "satisfactory," or "really poor," you may be able to work with him or her on preaching skills. Laypersons sometimes do not realize how clearly needed, and how deeply welcome, such support can be if it is substantive, gentle, and offered over time in the context of an ongoing personal relationship.

Frankly, if anything can be more discouraging than stinging criticism in a pastor's preaching ministry, it is the endless procession of "Nice sermon, pastor" comments the preacher has to endure at the back door after the service. Fed by no more than that, it is hardly surprising if, in time, even a good preaching ministry begins to shrivel.

Concentrated attention to what is involved in listening to preaching will eventually lead to questions about the sound, focus, and placement of your own preaching voice, even if you are not called to ordained ministry. In the following chapters we shall spend time reflecting on each of these matters. All of them, however, grow out of the central thrust: to talk substantially but non-technically about the preaching process. That means we will go first, as it were, "behind the scenes" to watch how sermons come to birth in the heart of an effective preacher.

2

More Than It Seems on the Surface

"That was a wonderful sermon!"

"I didn't think it was any good at all!"

HAT AN UNPROMISING START for a conversation! Where can it possibly go from there? "Concerning matters of taste there is no disputing," an ancient adage runs. I have talked about a hunger and an appetite for preaching, but underneath all that, is it possible that sermon quality is simply a matter of individual taste? Are attempts to analyze and evaluate sermons like trying to discuss whether or not liver is delicious?

Definitely not, some would say indignantly. Certain foods can be good for you whether you like them or not! There are objective criteria concerning food that nourishes. If you have a sweet tooth or a constant craving for junk food, for the sake of your health you need to re-educate your tastes. Even if everyone around you is into junk food, that won't make it nourishing.

Well, are there objective criteria for good preaching? If so, where shall we find them? Perhaps these criteria could come from the sort of definition one might find in a theological dictionary. Maybe that would help us zero in on what is distinctive and essential in preaching. Good sermons, then, would do what the theological dictionary says that they should.

Surely most of those who write such dictionaries would agree that preaching:

1) takes Scripture and Christian tradition as its starting point;

2) speaks to a community of faith (or invites listeners into such a community);

3) announces God's reconciling activity in Jesus Christ;

4) seeks to evoke repentance and transformation in the lives of those who hear.

A formal definition might go on to say that preaching is done only under particular circumstances (such as a church service), and only by individuals with certain credentials (such as ordination or a license).

Chances are your attention has already begun to wander as you make your way through this list, but if you are still on board, I suspect that something inside you is starting to grumble: "So what?"

Why? Perhaps you simply don't find such definitions interesting, but I suspect that the reason runs deeper. In all probability, much of the "bad" preaching you have suffered through fits quite comfortably inside the territory that my definition has marked out. Probably many of the preachers who deliver the sermons you find unappetizing would claim that they are doing just what the dictionary says they should. But as far as you are concerned, their sermons still miss the mark. The sense of good preaching we want cannot be supplied by a dictionary definition. So what do we need?

Maybe we would do better to approach from the back door. We could compile a list of all the things that have driven us up the wall and practically out of the church in the bad sermons we have heard. If we then replaced all those irritating qualities with their opposites, perhaps we would have a more helpful picture of what good preaching is.

On the other hand, it might be still more fruitful to begin positively, to recollect what has happened when we have been fortunate enough to hear good sermons. What do you remember about the experience of sermons you thought were effective? Maybe you were motivated to follow Christ into the suffering of the world, stimulated to study Scripture, challenged to pray or to witness. Maybe you suddenly connected for the first time with a character in a biblical story. (You simply couldn't identify with Mary at the wedding feast of Cana—a bossy busybody, both to her son and to the servants. But the preacher retold the story in a way that made you see both Mary's pain and her positive role in Jesus' early ministry.)

Perhaps you were touched by the preacher's obvious personal investment in the sermon, the congregation, or the outcasts of society. It was evident that the preacher really cared about what she was saying, about those to whom she was preaching, and about the unfortunate people whom it would be much more comfortable to ignore. Maybe the good sermons you remember presented unexpected insights that dislodged long-standing prejudices. (You had always felt superior to the Pharisees—and suddenly you realized, not only that the Pharisees were earnest about their religion, but also that you and they were related!) Maybe the sermons you found meaningful addressed a personal or social issue with which you had been wrestling, or which you needed to begin taking seriously. You rethought your responsibility to the chronically homeless and hungry, for example, in light of a particularly illuminating account of how Jesus dealt with the social outcasts of his day. Or maybe you came away from an inspiring sermon simply feeling closer to God.

On some occasions, however, what has moved you may have been the preacher's unusual accent, a beautiful church interior, or a stirring anthem by the choir. Perhaps you come to church in a more receptive mood on some Sundays than you do on others. Maybe, in fact, the hearts of sermon hearers are "strangely warmed" for reasons that escape them altogether, or that seem to have no connection with the preacher or the sermon. And it could well be that what your heart finds warming leaves other hearts cold.

Suddenly we are back to where we started: what makes a sermon good seems to be simply a matter of taste. At best, what we have in these reports of good preaching is a description of how we experience nourishment, not what makes sermons nourishing. If we want to understand preaching, therefore, it is no more helpful simply to call on our memories of sermons than it is to lay out a neat and tidy definition of preaching. Neither gives a satisfactory answer to the question: what goes into a good sermon?

Let's try to come at the question another way. Instead of thinking just about the sermon itself, or about the reactions it produces in us, why don't we try to see the preacher, the sermon, and the listener as intimately connected with each other? Suppose we see preaching as a verb instead of a noun, an activity instead of an object. This approach might make it more difficult to pin down the criteria for good preaching, but it might also open up some more concrete ways of looking at it.

This shift in orientation is easy enough to suggest, but difficult to do. If I ask you to describe the impressions that spontaneously leap to your mind when you hear the word "preaching," I would venture to guess most, if not all, of the following would emerge:

1) Someone is talking.

2) The speaker is delivering a monologue.

3) The monologue informs the assembled congregation about something it ought to know or to do.

4) Since the speaker knows that baldly ordering folks around is not likely to accomplish very much, language, personality, argument, and maybe even entertainment are all used to persuade the listeners.

5) The preacher presents a "product," a prepared and finished piece of work. (There is a manuscript, a set of notes, or at least a mental game plan.)

6) Because God's self-revelation in history is central to the Christian sermon, the preacher probably presents a report of God's saving acts recorded in Scripture as the basis of the sermon's exhortations.

Let's be even more concrete. There stands the preacher, alone in the pulpit. Everyone is paying attention without making a sound (except for those who are asleep, or a thousand miles away; except for small fry and rude folks who haven't learned yet that you don't talk when the preacher is talking). From a neat, computer printed manuscript, the preacher is giving a sermon on gratitude. He tells us how only one leper returned to thank Jesus for being healed. The preacher pronounces what he takes to be Jesus' judgment on the ninety percent who are ingrates. We must be like the one leper, not like the nine, he tells us. He throws in a couple of illustrations—one showing how good everyone feels when we remember to say "thank you," and the other underscoring how insensitive it is to forget to express gratitude. He may remind us that we owe our very existence to God, and that our new life in Christ is a free gift. A summary, an exhortation—"Can we do less than give and live our thanks for all we have been given?"—and at long last we get to stand and sing a hymn or say the creed.

The problem here is not just that the preacher was too busy, that he didn't work on the sermon long enough, or that he isn't very bright. The preacher has been following our description of preaching closely, but that description is superficial—quite literally, a view of the *surface* of preaching. The preacher who simply traces over such a surface will inevitably end up preaching sermons that are "flat." They may spark some interest here or there if the preacher hits upon a clever phrase, a vivid illustration, or some unanticipated point of contact with the listener's experience, but they are not likely to be richly nourishing over the long haul. Yet such sermons faithfully adhere to our definition of what preaching is.

A look below the surface of preaching, however, reveals something more; these "depth soundings" even appear in some respects to contradict the surface impressions I just listed. That is because the relationship between the heart of an effective sermon and what appears on its surface is in some ways similar to the relationship between a photographic negative and the picture that is ultimately produced from that negative.

A photographic negative is obviously different from a finished picture, yet without the negative there would be no picture. The negative outlines the shapes and patterns through which light passes as the print is exposed. The negative may appear to be only minimally related to the photograph; if anything, it looks like the opposite of the printed picture. Yet the negative makes the picture what it is. The quality of a picture will be only as good as the quality of its negative.

Photographs are fixed; preaching is much more fluid. Yet in a roughly similar way, there is a "negative" in good preaching that determines its "positive" outcome. There are characteristics in good preaching that, taken together, consistently produce the experience of spiritual nourishment—characteristics that may seem to be different from the surface impressions of preaching we have named.

Paradoxical though it may sound:

1) Preaching is much more a matter of listening than it is of speaking.

2) Preaching is far more a community interaction that it is an individual monologue.

3) Effective preaching is at root more descriptive of the human condition, and of the God who reaches toward that condition, than it is prescriptive about how we must, ought, or should think, feel, or act.

4) Good preaching evokes a response from listeners more than it exhorts them to respond.

5) Preaching is more continuing process than finished product, even if the sermon is written out and delivered verbatim.

6) Preaching is a creative action, not just a historical, theological, or scriptural report.

Each of these characteristics underlies good preaching. Although we may not immediately observe them in a sermon as it is delivered, they are the features through which effective preaching does its work. They make for preaching in which preacher, sermon, and listener are intimately connected. They make preaching an action rather than an object, a verb rather than a noun. In the rest of this chapter I want to address each of these underlying elements in more detail.

Preaching is more listening than speaking

Imagine a preacher who week after week rose to deliver a sermon, yet never uttered a word but only stood there, intently listening. Such a preacher would not occupy that pulpit for very long! Words must be spoken, obviously, if any preaching is to take place. Yet the preacher can speak only of what she has heard. Listening is more fundamental than speaking in the activity of preaching, so the most important task for any preacher is to become a good listener. The spoken word of the sermons is both an orchestration of, and a response to, the many voices to which good preachers are constantly listening.

Prior to preaching on any given Sunday, and in the very act of preaching itself, the preacher is listening to the texts of Scripture appointed for the day, and to scholarly and pastoral insights on the texts derived from reading and from conversation with others. The preacher is listening to the developing life stories of men and women in the congregation—to cries of confusion and pain in hospitals, to angry misunderstandings in troubled marriages, to struggles with moral dilemmas in the marketplace, to off-the-wall bantering from adolescents, to agonizing questions from college students encountering new and threatening worlds, to happy childhood chatter or the anxieties of the elderly.

She also listens to the hopeless cry of refugees from a civil war, to election campaign rhetoric, to stock market jitters, to rising unemployment rates, to cost-benefit questions in the health care delivery system, to the latest in contemporary music, to poetry, and to off-Broadway plays.

Preachers keep an ear tuned to theologians of the early church who are discussing the Trinity and the meaning of grace; they listen in on discussions among theologians like Barth, Tillich, and Bultmann. Effective preachers will also pay attention to thorny issues like inclusive language in Scripture and worship, to controversial questions concerning sexual expression—issues and questions that loom large in the denominational discussions of their churches. They also listen to very personal, individual, even private voices deep within themselves—voices of fear, hope, guilt, pain, satisfaction, fulfillment, and restlessness.

Even though the sermon is in some sense the preacher's creation, those who have practiced the art for any length of time will testify that sermons often tell their preachers the direction in which they need to go. Effective sermons are much more listened for than they are written, or "done," or worked up. And the sermon that the preacher hears during preparation must be listened to afresh as it is delivered.

The speaking of a sermon arises from listening to all kinds of voices. It is relatively easy for those in the pew to recognize a difference between a preacher who is constantly listening broadly and deeply, and one who listens, if at all, only to his own voice, or only to bits and snippets snatched from hurried, impatient conversations.

In and through, beneath and beyond all these voices, preachers are listening for the voice of God. But the God whom the preacher is attempting to hear is not simply a talking God. We worship a God who listens as well. "I have heard the cry of my people in Egypt," God tells Moses. If God listens before speaking, and then listens for a response as well, surely preachers can do no less!

Preaching is more of a community interaction than an individual monologue

From the fact that preaching is more listening than speaking, it follows naturally that preaching is not so much the solo speech of a particular individual as a conversation within the Christian community. The preacher, in other words, does not simply say "I hear you," and then respond with a timeless truth from Scripture. God's saving word is shaped to address the condition of the listeners in their various contexts, and is uttered in dialogue with them.

Preaching is more than speaking *to* a congregation, however sensitively; it is speaking *for* and *with* a congregation as well. Preaching attempts to articulate the concerns, questions, commitments, and celebrations of the whole faith community. "How long will you hide yourself, O Lord?" cries the psalmist. Sometimes the preacher echoes a similar heartfelt cry on behalf of the congregation; at other times the sentiment may be quite different: "Your love, O Lord, forever will I sing."

Sometimes insights from members of the congregation will express what a preacher has no words for. I recently heard a preacher describe her experience with a group of children who were trying to construct an altar frontal for the season of Epiphany. All the standard "wise men bearing gifts" scenes were discussed and discarded. Out of a frustrated silence came a suggestion from a fragile little girl who lived in a family deeply enmeshed in emotional disturbance. "I think the gift the wise men left with was more valuable than the presents they brought," she said. That insight became the basis of the altar frontal and the centerpiece of the preacher's powerful sermon on John 3:16.

So the preacher not only listens and responds to the voices she hears, but also brings those voices to life in the sermon. The sermon is not a monologue, but an unfolding conversation of the people of God—a conversation about and with God, and about their struggles to know and be faithful to God.

But the conversation does not stop there. In addition to resonating with the conversations that go on throughout the week in the parish community, preaching brings in voices that otherwise might be neglected or ignored—voices of the oppressed, of those who see God from a different perspective or in a different cultural light. It gives voice to those who have gone before us in Christian tradition, so that we will not be denied the benefit of their hardwon wisdom. Good preaching will not close its ears even to voices outside the Christian tradition. Although sometimes unfamiliar, jarring, or antagonistic, these voices may have a prophetic word that will prevent a community from becoming too closed in upon itself.

The wider the perspectives that are invited into the preaching conversation, the healthier the community (and the preaching) is likely to be. All voices cannot be heard simultaneously, of course. But voices heard in the preparation for preaching can be consistently excluded only at the community's peril. Conversations sound very different, depending upon the voices that participate in them.

An up-and-coming young executive, for example, feels he is "suffering as a Christian" because he has received a lower salary increase than he thought he had coming. How does his complaining sound in the presence of someone who has been consistently discriminated against, and denied any job at all? Bring a woman trapped in an abusive marriage into the preaching conversation, and discussions about how wives are to be "submissive" to their husbands cannot help but take on a different tone.

Inviting them into the discussion will complicate it immeasurably, but that is better than talking to ourselves. Conversation—with prophets, apostles, martyrs, young executives, battered wives, and all the company of heaven—is the "negative" through which the God who is Trinity communicates with those who are listening. Preaching is more of a community interaction than an individual monologue. The preacher delivering a sermon may appear to be a solitary person making a speech, but preaching is more than it seems on the surface.

Preaching is more descriptive than prescriptive

Because superficial impressions of preaching are so widespread, the word itself quickly conjures up in the popular mind the image of a moral lecture, a heavy-handed reprimand issued in the name of an offended authority figure. It is hardly surprising that most people have little time for such sermons: "How dare you preach to me like that!" "Your sermon was kind of preachy!"

Some Scripture passages, lifted from their contexts, can be pressed into the service of that common assumption. ("Woe to you, scribes and Pharisees, hypocrites!") There are many preachers who consider it their business to tell people how God demands that they behave—or else. Such sermons, however, skew the underlying shape of good preaching and distort the shape of the Gospel.

Preaching is fundamentally descriptive. The primary business of preaching, if it follows the broad but clear contours of Holy Scripture, is to announce what *is*, rather than to hassle listeners about what *should* be.

Scripture describes the world with clear accuracy—its beauty, its harshness, its ambiguity. It is similarly perceptive concerning human behavior—its naivete, its yearning for goodness, its moral achievements, its tragic and malicious failures, its woundedness and fragility. In vivid metaphors, Holy Writ ventures to describe the indescribable—the majesty and mercy of the divine. With stories and ideas the Bible describes the drama of God's reconciling love revealed in history and in the life, death, and resurrection of Jesus Christ. We are constantly confronted in Scripture with the promise of accepting and the peril of refusing so great a salvation.

Together, these descriptions illustrate and illuminate—they do not impose, extort, or browbeat. Prophetic announcements that appear to be sheer condemnation are always attempts to dispel blindness, to upset complacency so that the hearers can see things as they really are. Sometimes the threat of a disintegrating future produces its intended effect of repentance and transformation, as in the unwilling prophecy of Jonah that averts the destruction of Nineveh. Sometimes the warnings are not heeded, and the descriptions are proven all too true: listen to the bone-chilling description of the fall of Jerusalem recorded in 2 Chronicles 36:14-21.

When it is effective, preaching will make its announcement with imaginative accuracy, creating a space for the Holy Spirit to do its own persuading. Preaching will provide a response to the question, "What must I do to be saved?"; God and the listener do the rest. Preachers can neither force God's word down throats, nor put words in the mouths of those who need to respond. By going straight to the imperative—to what must be done—preachers take upon themselves what is God's business, not theirs. By describing the way things are, the preacher enables the congregation to hear and respond to what God requires. Any sense of obligation to God can only arise from a more fundamental understanding of who God is and how God engages us as we are.

Time and time again, in sermons delivered both by seminarians and by seasoned parish priests, I have heard the preacher rail against the flaws and foibles of them, or you, or us. The effect on hearers is predictably one of three: 1) an increased load of anxiety and guilt (which sticks far more effectively than the announcement of the Good News, for which the "bad news" was supposedly a set-up); 2) a deep and bitter resentment, reinforcing the hearer's negative impression of preaching; or 3) an emotional distancing and an intellectual check-out from whatever the preacher is saying.

In preaching classes, where it is my business to address both the issue and the preacher, I could easily launch into a broadside about how sermons must, ought, and should not harp on must, ought, and should. That teaching strategy, however, is as unnecessary as it is counter-productive. Once we begin to talk about "preachy" sermons, the problem becomes easily apparent. Careful analysis of the sermons in question almost always reveals that heavy-handed prescriptions have been pressed into service as a substitute for images, narratives, or arguments that clearly and convincingly describe the human condition and the grace of God. "We must...we ought...we should..." rush in to fill the vacuum created by failing to think out and to express articulately and imaginatively who we are, what God has revealed about the divine character, what the world is like, and how God promises to transform it.

Preaching evokes our response more than it exhorts us to respond

If people do not automatically assume that preaching is a put-down, they may envision the sermon in terms of a pep rally—an attempt to work up the faithful, to urge them to pray, to give, to study, to undertake efforts on behalf of the less fortunate, or to do other things righteous and religious. Preaching does what political campaigning does: incite and re-energize those who are already true believers. If that assumption is correct, the main difference between the two is that political campaigning by and large does its job more effectively.

It is difficult to disagree with this assessment when you compare the respective surfaces of much preaching and almost all political campaigning. The preacher who primarily exhorts, however, always risks falling into a Pelagian trap. If we cannot pull ourselves up by our own bootstraps, neither can we pull up any one else. If anything is ultimately to be effective in transforming us, it will only be the love of God. Those who hear the message of divine love will have to recognize it as already at work upon and within them. The preacher's task is to name what is already present, to evoke it, to call it forth, rather than to lay it on or crank it up.

High-powered exhortations tend, upon repeated application, to lose their power of jolting us into action. Once the sermon hearers have had their circuits burned, it may prove impossible for future exhortations to extract any more from them. More important, it will be very difficult to help them discover the healing and energizing grace that has been about them all the time, awaiting recognition.

To use evocative speech requires discipline of thought, language, and imagination; wooing is more subtle, less efficient, and more ambiguous than giving orders. But when preachers have faith in the loving, persuasive power of God, they choose strategies that evoke rather than exhort, and offer rather than order.

Preaching is more of a continuing process than a finished product

When does preparation for any particular sermon actually begin? The first reading of the Scriptures appointed is probably as definable a point as any. But the situation is in fact much less clear-cut than that. My whole life, I discover, is preparatory work for each sermon I preach. Different aspects of my life experience, in surprising but very explicit ways, emerge in the context of my formal preparation, and let me know quite emphatically that what I *thought* was the beginning of preparation for a sermon was actually the middle of the journey.

When is a sermon "done"? When the pen is put down or the computer printer is turned off? Certainly not—it isn't a sermon until it is preached! Is the sermon finished when at last there is silence in the sanctuary after the concluding sentence has sounded forth? No, for then the most important work of the sermon has only just begun. The sermon enters ongoing conversations in the minds and hearts of the listeners, and starts to reshape the directions of their lives. For example, a sermon titled, "Jesus and Our Wounds," which I heard at a most vulnerable time in my life, has led, gently but inexorably, over a period of more than fifteen years, to a change in my vocation, even though neither the sermon nor the reasons it was meaningful at the time have any obvious connection with my current work as a teacher of preaching.

Words used in a sermon may help focus a preacher, and may be used by a preacher to focus an insight or a sense of direction for the congregation. But the ending of a sermon is never a still point, a freeze-dried timeless truth captured and dispatched. Good sermons are never scattered, vague, or half-baked; they are open-ended, designed to be catalysts and springboards.

Preaching is more creative action than historical report

In our eagerness to bear witness to God's saving deeds experienced in history and recorded in Scripture, we can lose sight of the fact that the point of preaching is transformation, not an account of transformation coupled with an order to "go get transformed."

Recent philosophers have coined the term "performative utterance" to describe a particular function of our language. Phrases like: "The meeting is adjourned," "I pronounce that they are husband and wife," "I promise to give you $500," and "You are forgiven," are unusual statements. They do not report facts, define terms, issue commands, or express feelings. They produce what they proclaim; they are acts in themselves. They are words that "do things."

The opening chapters of Genesis describe God creating the cosmos through a series of speech-acts. The Incarnation, the Word made flesh, was God's speech-act formed in body language. Gospel proclamation is itself a "mighty act of God." Preaching extends this mighty act in performative utterances; it does not just report on what God did "once upon a time."

The title of a recent book by the retired Archbishop of Canterbury, Donald Coggin, is *Preaching: The Sacrament of the Word*, which succinctly captures this dimension of preaching. Effective preaching is not merely a series of words or reports; instead, it is intended by God as an actual creative extension of the Word of Life.

In catholic tradition, the sacraments of the church, through word and gesture, achieve what they symbolically announce. Holy water used in baptism, while set apart for sacred use, is an everyday element all the same. The reality of Real Presence in the eucharist does not subvert the organic composition of bread and wine. The Word made flesh was flesh indeed. All of these perfectly natural elements, touched by grace, are transformed and do transform. Similarly, the words of preaching are merely, fully, human words. Yet, engraced by the Word, they actually accomplish the salvation they announce.

The six characteristics I have just described are critical in effective preaching. I have described them as "negatives" to indicate that they function in preaching in a way that is somewhat analogous to the way a photographic negative defines the picture. These dimensions of preaching are not always readily apparent to us, yet preaching shaped in accordance with them resonates with authenticity. When grounded in Christian theology, they accord, I believe, with the deepest hungers of our human experience. Sermons that are superficial, that lack these underlying elements, may *sound* like preaching. They may even strike some hearers as "powerful"; but they will not satisfy for long our yearning for nourishment from the word of God. While such sermons may manipulate, they seldom transform.

Thus far I have been talking very broadly about preaching. In the second part of this book, we will look in closer detail at the way in which the preaching process actually develops. The first two characteristics—preaching as listening and dialogue—will be addressed more substantively in chapter three. Chapter four shows how preaching can effectively describe and evoke, while chapter five takes up that aspect of preaching known as "performative utterance."

Essential Tasks In Shaping Sermons

3

Engaging the Various Voices

"IF YOU WANT THE JOB done right, get a professional." Your family may swear by Great-Aunt Martha's home-brewed stomach remedy, but if you suspect appendicitis, you don't reach for the bottle, you call for a surgeon. You may enjoy puttering around as an amateur plumber, but when the last turn of your wrench on the hot water pipe sends up a geyser that all but floats your house away, you know it's time to call a *real* plumber!

We live in a society where job specialization is the norm. Mechanics, stock brokers, carpenters, and teachers are specially trained and certified to undertake the services they provide. Within their respective specialties they are "professionals"; outside of these areas, they have no special authority. It can be socially unacceptable, illegal, and even dangerous to wander onto the turf of other professionals.

Each profession has its own special tools, techniques, and vocabularies that are all but unintelligible to outsiders. The benefits professionals offer us are closely tied to the sophisticated apparatus, methods, and language they use. We regard professional services as indispensable, but there is a down side to all this specialization, too. If your stomach is cramping badly, or your automobile engine is gasping and sputtering, it is a great relief to have someone available who can figure out the problem and fix it. But how helpless and frustrating it feels when the internist or the mechanic starts talking to you about your stomach or your carburetor in language you cannot understand! You respect the need for technical jargon, but you wish profoundly that the professionals could talk with you on your own level.

A similar dynamic sometimes holds between parishioners and preachers. We don't believe just anybody should get up to preach—we expect our preachers to be talented and trained. We allow them their professional jargon. It would be presumptuous to tell them their business, much less to meddle in it. All the same, however, we want them to preach to us in language we can understand!

But to what extent is it accurate to describe a preacher as a professional? The basic aptitudes we look for do not seem to be the kinds of unusual abilities that are essential for an athlete, musician, scientist, or an expert technician. Basic intelligence, facility in public speaking, a pleasing personality, interest in people, and reasonable skills in organization seem sufficient for a budding preacher. We do look for evidence of Christian commitment, maturity, and interest in continuing religious education in our preachers, but we value and nurture these qualities in everyone who takes the church seriously.

This might suggest that there is nothing particularly special about what it takes to be a preacher. And there is important truth in that suggestion, because preachers are not professionals in precisely the same way as other specialists. Preachers and parishioners alike are engaged in a common venture of listening, through many ears, to the God who addresses us all. Preachers have no automatic claim to special revelation or status.

Yet our churches do specifically school and ordain preachers, based on some evidence of their vocational "promise." We sense intuitively that certain individuals would "do well" as preachers (and that others would do everyone a favor by finding another job). But what kind of "professionalism" are we looking for? To put the matter more bluntly, if there aren't any distinguishing marks that we can see before candidates go into seminary, what do we expect to be different about their preaching when they come out?

The distinctively professional dimensions of preaching have to do with theological training—special competence in the study of Scripture, theology, church history, and other related disciplines. The doctor or mechanic is able to look at the same human body or automobile engine that we see and draw our attention to things that we don't immediately observe. The preacher should be able to do something similar with Scripture, liturgy, and with religious writing and experience generally. We expect preachers to speak about the human condition before God with insight, and to make diagnoses, prescriptions, and prognoses of human problems from a theological perspective. In a word, the preacher should show credentials in the analysis of the Scriptures and other sources that will lead to responsible theological explanation.

The opening of John's gospel, for example, has words upon words about the Word. We may know, from having heard it countless times, that the Word which became flesh and dwelt among us is Jesus. But why doesn't the author just say so and be done with it? What does all that "Word" business have to say to people who live in a society where words tend to be means of manipulation, or are reducible to bytes and bits in a vast information-processing network? We may have some ideas of our own about what it means for Jesus to be the Word; we do not want the preacher to spoon-feed us. But we certainly could use some help in understanding what it meant to the gospel writer to talk about Jesus that way, and what Jesus as the Word might mean for us.

So far, so good. But now a problem arises. By learning a theological vocabulary, the preacher will be able to tell us a number of things about "logos christology." In doing so, however, the preacher will run the risk of generating the kind of frustration that a physician or a mechanic does when describing our stomach or our automobile engine accurately but (to us) unintelligibly.

You don't have to listen in a given congregation very long to hear sharply conflicting opinions concerning the preacher's professional domain:

1) "Who are we to tell the preacher what to say? That isn't our business. We must pray for the preacher, and trust that somehow the preaching we hear will be good for us. After all, we are only laypeople."

2) "God speaks to all of us, not just to the preacher. The church should not knuckle under to the culture of professionalism. We don't need a religious professional to talk to God, and we don't have to depend upon a religious professional to hear what God is saying to us. Sermons are fine, as long as they speak to us where we are. They give us no more, and no less, than we can get through private or small group Bible study."

3) "The world the preacher talks about is long ago and far away. It isn't relevant. It's fine if our preacher wants to go off and do scholarly research, but that's not what we're paying a salary for!"

Those who occupy the pulpit often experience similar anxieties about their professional preparation:

1) "How can I ever do enough research to justify the message I am supposed to preach? I can't hold a candle to the *really* professional scholars, and with the other pressing demands of the parish, I'll never manage to get good enough. How can I possibly preach?"

2) "Even if I could make it to the big leagues, who would listen to the heavy erudition I would end up preaching? And who needs to? Wouldn't it be better simply to open the word of God and trust that, listening together, we will hear God's message for us emerging in the midst of our common experience?"

3) "There is so much fascinating stuff to discover in studying the biblical world. What a shame that I am always having to draw up short, and think about a sermon! Maybe I should chuck parish ministry and take up teaching theology in graduate school."

The underlying questions beneath all these opinions, of course, have to do with the relation between the professional and the layperson in the community of faith. In what sense is it not only acceptable but essential for the preacher to operate as a professional? To what extent should the preacher be seen as a specialist? Putting the question in terms of the New Testament's discussion of different gifts in the Body of Christ, how can preachers and parishioners exercise their callings in ways that honor the distinctiveness of their respective roles? How can each contribute to building up the church in unity and maturity in Christ?

A way of addressing these questions has already been suggested in the last chapter. The speaking that is the surface of preaching is shaped by the listening that underlies it, and this listening occurs in the context of a *conversation*. The most important task of any preacher is to become a good listener. Formal theological training enables the preacher to engage in what the profession calls "exegesis." Exegesis, however, can be understood as the process of using certain methods designed to facilitate careful and systematic listening.

How, then, can the listening of preacher and parishioner, of professional and layperson, be understood in mutually enriching and challenging ways? In light of this question I want to return to some of the different dimensions of listening that were quickly surveyed in the last chapter: listening to voices 1) in the Scriptures, 2) in the congregation, 3) in the cultural environment, 4) in the liturgy, and 5) within the preacher. Both preachers and parishioners can make distinctive contributions to listening in all these ways, and this listening will provide the sources from which consistently nourishing sermons are shaped. Carefully engaging these voices in conversation is the first essential stage in the task of preparing to preach.

Listening to voices in the Scriptures

The kind of immediate, first-impression listening that both preacher and congregation give to a biblical text is very important in its own right. It cannot be sidestepped in a rush to drag out the professional apparatus. Competent professionals always listen carefully to the descriptions that come from non-professionals: the first thing your doctor or mechanic does is ask you what the symptoms are. Professional listening on the part of the preacher does not tell laypersons they did not hear anything worth paying attention to. The task of preachers is to help in broadening and deepening the meaning of those first reports, as well as to make new, distinctive observations.

If there is a problem with spontaneous, untrained reflections on a text of Scripture, it is that lay listeners may not grasp the context—the larger whole, the bigger picture. They may not be aware of the ongoing conversation of which a particular passage is merely one part.

When the writer of Ezekiel claims, for example, "Everyone shall die for their own sin," he is in dialogue with a long-standing tradition of belief in Israel's corporate responsibility that derives from its covenant relationship with God. Speaking to a people now in exile, the prophet is reacting against a view of community solidarity that has gone to seed—"We are being punished for our ancestors' wrongdoings, and there is nothing we can do about our fate!" "No," says the prophet, "there is another side to the covenant relationship. God both honors and requires individual righteousness!"

In his letter to the Galatians, Paul constructs an argument about the relation of law and grace which sounds all but irrational to contemporary ears. He drags in Abraham, Hagar, Sarah, and Isaac in a way that sounds like absent-minded free association. One can hardly have a clue as to what is going on here without some understanding of the Hebrew tradition of interpreting Scripture.

So we are always breaking into some conversation whenever we begin to read a text of Scripture, regardless of where we start, just as we always leave the conversation partway through. Entering the conversations of Scripture is similar to entering any other: if we come into the middle of a conversation and at once announce its "meaning," we run the risk of making fools of ourselves, and a shambles of the conversation—even if we think we know exactly what everyone is talking about. Instead, we have to pause, listen, and get our bearings. While we can say "what this conversation means to me" if we want to, we need to realize that the connection between what we pick up and what is actually going on may be tenuous at best!

What a congregation needs a well-prepared preacher to do is to encourage them in richer, deeper listening through the specialized techniques of theological training. Texts of Scripture must be heard, so far as possible, in the historical and cultural contexts in which they were first recorded, composed, or edited. Listeners to a sermon are entitled to understand what was going on in the conversations of their spiritual ancestors if they are to understand themselves as a part of the family of God.

It is possible, for instance, to derive inspiration and insight from a first-hand reading of chapters 4-10 in the letter to the Hebrews, which talk about Jesus as the Great High Priest. To know that Jesus identifies with our struggles, wounds, and shortcomings is certainly comforting. But how much more meaningful still it can be to grasp this compassion in the context in which the letter was apparently written—to a discouraged and fearful group of Christians worn down by misunderstanding and persecution. For us to hear that Jesus is a priest may conjure up images of him in a chasuble (especially since the image is reinforced by many carved statues situated above church altars). It is something else again to catch a sense of the rich allusions to Jewish priesthood that are caught up and transfigured in Jesus' life, death, and resurrection. Who we are as a Christian community is profoundly affected by our understanding of how Jesus is our priest, and how his priesthood has been understood in the life of earlier Christian communities.

Scriptural exegesis—professional listening to Scripture—can seem a daunting undertaking. There are many different texts in the collection we call Holy Scripture, written at different times in different places for different purposes by different authors. Many texts consciously refer to, incorporate, elaborate, or modify the thrust of other texts. The prophet Habakkuk, for example, says that "the righteous live by their faith." Against the ominous backdrop of threatening Babylonian power, the author is wrestling with the perennial question of how God can allow the righteous to suffer and the wicked to prosper. Later Paul picks up the same phrase in his letter to the Galatians, but he uses it differently. Paul is arguing that it is faith in Christ, not the following of any law, that sets us in right relationship with God.

What the preacher must avoid is the tendency to assume that, because all of the books in Scripture have been officially incorporated into what we call "The Bible," they present a single, thoroughly consistent set of definitive "truths" needing only to be dug out of their various contexts, assembled in a neat package, and wrapped up with contemporary relevance. Many distinctive voices speak in Scripture. Different gospel writers not only describe different incidents in Jesus' ministry, they present distinctive—even divergent—accounts of the same incidents. The cleansing of the temple appears at the beginning of Jesus' ministry in the Gospel of John; the other three gospels place it at the end. Luke's account reads as though it might have been Jesus' words alone that drove the money changers out; Mark and Matthew have Jesus getting overtly physical. The most plausible explanation for this divergence is not that the facts were in dispute, but that different authors heard stories of Jesus in different contexts, and addressed the Word of Life as they heard it to the different needs of different listening communities.

God is apparently patient with the diversity, ambiguity, and even conflict that one finds in the voices of Scripture; good preachers will be patient as well, or lose much of the richness and realism of Scripture. Still, when we open a Bible (especially a new one with clear, easy-to-read typeface, crinkly pages, and soft, sweet-smelling covers), it is difficult to keep in mind how many different voices and situations are compressed into what appears as one book, each section and chapter following the last in regular succession.

Perhaps it is easier to understanding how the preacher must listen if we imagine ourselves gathered to hear the recording of a long and significant dramatic reading. Soon we become aware that, even though the recording and the player are state-of-the-art, the recording itself is very old. Although they do not always stop to identify themselves, there are obviously several speakers communicating in a number of different genres. They tell stories, sing songs, construct arguments, express ecstasy and outrage, issue commands, and offer good advice in the form of wise sayings.

From the sound of the recording it is obvious that some of the transcriptions are fuzzy—we cannot always make out what is being said. When we listen more closely, we can hear that some of the segments of the recording have been composed by piecing together still more ancient recordings. While much of the transcription is clear enough, the meaning of many words, phrases, and ideas is still unclear. Those of us who listen have very different understandings of what we have heard. We quickly realize that, unless we have sources of information other than the recording itself, we will not be able to discern the meaning of the words as used by the original speakers.

We also notice that certain distinctive speech forms keep recurring. After turning off the tape, we wonder what social pressures the speakers were responding to or what social norms they were trying to define. We also sense that more has been going on than the straightforward addressing of important issues, or the reporting of significant events. The material we have heard has been woven into subtle literary plots and structures of which we have only the faintest of notions.

Suppose, after this intensive listening exercise, when all these different dimensions have been opened up for us, someone comes in late, huffing and puffing. "What does the recording say?" he demands, obviously interested in a no-frills answer. The question is intelligible; but so would be our hesitation to fire off the kind of response he wants to hear. Both he and we need some professional help with this recording.

In an analogous way, we need help with careful listening to the Scriptures. That is why preachers use various professional strategies, such as *text criticism*, which is an attempt to get at the most reliable manuscript available, and *source criticism*, which attempts to find where the materials have come from. *Historical criticism* is a strategy that tries to answer questions about the social and historical setting in which the words of Scripture were spoken and written down—the context that is essential for discovering their original meaning. *Form criticism* tries to identify a connection between particular life situations and distinctive speech patterns that frequently recur in Scripture texts. Questions about how those who tell Scripture's story edit their materials to make them serve their particular purposes are addressed by *redaction criticism*. *Sociological criticism* asks how the text itself expresses and challenges social arrangements in light of the authors' understanding of God's revelation. Finally, *literary criticism* investigates how the message of that revelation is distinctively embodied in the various literary forms of the text.

None of these strategies is an attempt to "criticize" the text, in the sense of passing judgment on whether or not it speaks truly. Rather, these are methods for systematic listening to Scripture so that we will be better able to understand how God's word comes to us truly and distinctively in any given passage.

How might some of these strategies assist the sermon preparation of a listening preacher?

Suppose the task is a sermon for Easter Day from the Gospel of Mark. The consensus of *text critics* is that the best manuscripts of Mark's gospel end with "So they went out and fled from the tomb, for terror and amazement had seized them; and they said nothing to anyone, for they were afraid." Verses 9-19 seem to be the work of a different writer. To preach a resurrection that is stark, unsettling, even terrifying to its witnesses— which is what the most reliable text suggests—presents some important possibilities for Easter preaching that do not appear in the resurrection accounts of the other gospels. When the Easter text is drawn from Mark, there is great value in letting the congregation hear his distinctive account.

One cannot read the gospels without the impression that Jesus is always getting into arguments with the religious leaders of his day. *Form critics* recognize a recurrent pattern of "controversy stories" in the gospels, and suggest that such stories may have been devices used by the authors to set forth, in dramatic fashion, conflicts that early believers were encountering in the society in which they were living and attempting to witness. In the second chapter of Mark, for example, Jesus is presented as defending the grain-plucking of his disciples against the charge of sabbath violation by local Pharisees. The issue of religious custom versus deeper human need is neatly framed by the story, which leads to Jesus' saying: "The sabbath was made for humankind, and not humankind for the sabbath"(2:27).[1] Knowing how the form of a controversy story functioned for biblical writers in their own community, a preacher today could focus on how the modern church may seriously misunderstand the freedom Jesus enjoins. How odd if, feeling freed from religious rules by Jesus' saying about the sabbath, we joined the

crowds in a Sunday trip to the shopping mall, when this might
be the very kind of behavior from which we desperately need release! We might do better to take a sabbath rest, suspending
business as usual in favor of quiet meditation and works of
mercy.

Walter Brueggemann, an outstanding scholar of the Hebrew
Scriptures, illustrates the integration of *source, historical, redaction, literary,* and *sociological* methods of exegesis in a sermon titled, "A Footnote to the Royal Pageant," based on the eighth
chapter of 1 Kings, which describes the dedication of Solo-
mon's temple. Listening to this narrative, Brueggemann's ear
discerns three different sources, each from a different historical
period, and each with a distinctive agenda. Verses 12-13 repre-
sent, he thinks, "uncompromising, uncritical temple theology"—
a theology which believes, in effect, that the voice of the
royal-religious establishment is the voice of God. Verses 27-30,
however, contain a theology from later writers that critiques this
"God and country" theology. After verse 30, an even later perspective emerges from the period of the exile, that, while still
critical of temple theology, attempts to affirm certain elements
of the naive trust it contains.

How to make all these conflicting voices come together in a
sermon? Brueggemann constructs a scenario in which different
characters react to the elaborate pomp and spectacle of the temple dedication liturgy. There is a prophet who thunders against
the self-serving idolatry of identifying YHWH with the domi-
nant social structure; there is a temple custodian on post-liturgy
cleanup detail who has little use for either royal pageantry or
prophetic sociological critique, but who recognizes a responsibility to follow God's law; there is also a beaten and powerless
old woman who comes to the temple, clinging to an assurance
that, in the temple, God is there for her. All these characters

are allowed space in the sermon. It is evident that, with respect to those in the various strata of society, and in various states of self-sufficiency, God afflicts the comfortable and comforts the afflicted. Brueggemann concludes:

> Our struggle with the God of the Bible is that God's presence is real, but never on our terms. In God's presence we are more surprised than assured, more shattered than accepted. But how we meet God turns out to be a gift from God, never designed by us. ...We have the text, the temple, the tablets, the ark, the liturgy. Our life-work is in sorting it out. The royal pageant is important. But God is not a mere footnote.[2]

Few preachers, particularly those who preach Sunday after Sunday, will have the time or the expertise to do such a sophisticated textual listening as Brueggemann does in this sermon. A conscientious preacher, though, will endeavor to make use of all of these listening strategies in attempting to hear the word of God in Scripture with and for the congregation.

Use of these strategies in the preparation of the sermon is not the same as reference to them in the sermon itself. An author may craft a short story, essay, or drama according to certain literary principles that a careful reader might detect, but the author will seldom allude to these in the work itself. Similarly, the sermon will not normally draw attention to the methods that have been used in listening for it; they are *means* to a fresh hearing, not *ends in themselves*. So if the preacher practices professional listening with rigor and reverence, what we will hear in the sermon is not an impressive set of techniques, nor a jargon-laden research report. Rather, we will hear a clear, simple, relevant word of the Lord—a word that nourishes, liberates, challenges, empowers, and transforms.

Demanding and absorbing though it is, listening to Scripture is not the only professional task of the preacher. Scripture must be heard in concert with other voices that require careful attention as well.

Listening to voices in the congregation

Listening to a congregation does not mean that the preacher will try to figure out what the people want to hear. Nor does it mean that members of a congregation will be shocked by (or apprehensive about) the use of personal confessions or life secrets from the pulpit. A preacher does not listen to parishioners in order to seek out foibles against which to rail, anonymously and in the abstract. Rather, in regular parish activities, casual conversations, and formal appointments, preachers listen for the heartbeat of the parish—its fears, hopes, joys, stresses, blind spots; its rough and cutting edges. If this listening is intent and ongoing, a preacher will be able to offer a relevant word in a moment of crisis, as well as to draw attention to subtle shifts in parish mood and direction that need to be encouraged or held up to scrutiny.

In listening professionally to a congregation, a preacher does not set out to glean timely sermon topics or snappy illustrations. The people with whom a preacher lives and works are worth listening to just because they are who they are. We will become suspicious and resentful if we get the sense that our preacher is eavesdropping, or using our conversations as "sermon fodder." The ongoing conversations of the congregation have their own integrity; they do not exist simply for the sake of preaching, even though the preacher must be tuned into them in order to speak a relevant word.

As a preacher's kid, I was sometimes embarrassed at the way stories of life in my family found their way, without warning, into my father's sermons. It wasn't that the stories made me look particularly bad; it was rather that my life was not my own, or at least I never knew what parts of my life were suddenly going to turn into public property. Eventually we held a family council on the matter. It is amazing what a difference it made when we agreed that my father would not use family life material without asking us first. What I had previously dreaded I now actually began to enjoy.

If we clearly understand that the intention of our preacher's listening is the celebration of community, as well as its nurture—if that listening helps us voice our common concerns before God, if it brings the presence of God into the activities of our lives—then we will be willing to join in a conversation that can find its place in the wider conversation of preaching. More than willing, we will eagerly anticipate the ways in which our contributions will be woven into the total fabric of preaching from week to week.

Preachers, insecure about whether their congregations regard them as worth listening to, sometimes think that they must be not only original in thought and expression, but clandestine in sermon preparation as well. To talk about what one was preparing to preach would be to "steal one's own thunder," or to "let the cat out of the bag." It is almost as if they think that the success of the sermon depends on something like keeping the punch line of a joke under cover until the right moment to spring it forth. But such fears betray the conviction that preaching is a monologue, which, as we have seen, is a misguided and superficial understanding.

In this regard, one of my most exciting and nourishing preaching experiences involved group preparation for a sermon delivered at a church conference. All of us worked with the Scriptures together, listening to each other's insights and concerns, and agreeing on topics the sermon should address. We discussed at length how God seemed to be addressing us through the Scriptures. While it might seem that there would be nothing left to say, and that the formal sermon would inevitably be anti-climactic, precisely the opposite occurred. The intensity of everyone's participation in the sermon was palpable. While the organizational development, images, and sentence constructions of the sermon were my own, the meaning had come forth from the shared dialogue of the community. Furthermore, when articulated in the sermon, that meaning re-engaged us all with more depth and power than it probably could have if each one of us had come to the sermon independently. My overwhelming impression was that, though such a preparation procedure might not be feasible on a regular basis, it was nevertheless the ideal—an ideal that could be approached in practical ways if consciously attended to by both preacher and congregation. Preaching is not merely directed *to* a congregation, but it speaks *for* and *with* them.

Listening to voices in the cultural environment

We are powerfully affected by international conflicts, domestic political debates, social, economic, and ecological problems, as well as by movements in literature, drama, music, and the visual arts. Yet I wonder how many people listened to sermons delivered on the Sunday after the beginning of the war with Iraq that made no mention of it. I wonder how many young people conclude, almost without realizing it, that God is irrelevant to them because the music to which they listen, the peer pressure they constantly encounter, the athletic events they attend, and the drugs they are offered are never even acknowledged in preaching.

As a society becomes more complicated, fragmented, and prone to violence and disaster, most of us tend instinctively to withdraw from what we find distasteful and overwhelming, even though we continue to be affected by it. Human need, greed, cynical exploitation, desperate self-protecting interest, insensitivity to systemic injustice, and tragic choices are more pervasive than we can begin to cope with. Therefore, the Gospel and the church can seem to us safe havens from cultural pressures, rather than the means through which God engages the world and calls us to make contact with it. The same filters that enable us to keep out the waves of ambiguity and suffering around us also cut us off from epiphanies of beauty, self-sacrifice, and poetic insight that are all around us as well. If we shut out the tragedy of disease and poverty, we will cut ourselves off from important spiritual nourishment that comes only from direct experience of the faith and courage evident among those who, through grace, live in the midst of such tragedies.

Preachers are often tempted to sift through bits and pieces of cultural data, casting about in search of titles, catch phrases, or plugs for the sermon. Simply to refer to "a thousand points of light," rap music, the faith of a dying cancer patient, rising murder rates, or current unemployment statistics in a sermon does not automatically give the sermon relevance. Such simplistic listening can hardly be called professional, and its results sound contrived. Occasionally the right newsclip, image, phrase, or human interest story will find its way into the sermon. When these are effective, however, it is not because they are interest-grabbing tidbits, but because they serve as metaphors for perceiving realities much bigger than the image, slogan, or story itself.

In ordinary conversations it is relatively easy to tell how someone is listening to us. There is a world of difference between listeners who scan what we say in search of what they want to hear and listeners who attempt to enter into the world of our experience, regardless of whether or not they see matters the way we do. Good listening for preaching is the latter kind.

Preachers and congregations together need to listen to the world as it presents itself to us, and not as we wish it to be, or as we are convinced on other grounds (even theological grounds) that it must be. The most effective resonance between Scripture, the experience of the congregation, and the current conditions of society will be one in which none of these voices is allowed either to drown out the others or to decide what the others are really saying. Instruments cannot be orchestrated if they cannot be heard, or if some instruments are allowed only to echo others.

The importance of listening both to congregational and cultural voices was recently brought home to me quite forcefully. As a result of gentle but clear observations by a woman in a recent preaching course, I will no longer use as an example of good preaching a particular sermon by a highly regarded preacher. This sermon is substantive and original in its scriptural exegesis, and dazzling in its imagistic recreation of one of Jesus' parables, but it makes incidental yet uncritical references to prostitution. It does so in a way that subtly (and probably unconsciously) reinforces sexist views of women and simplistic presumptions about this complex social evil. Focusing as I did on the ways in which the sermon listens to Scripture, I missed the way it profoundly failed to listen to the world around us. I saw clearly, after it had been pointed out to me, that it takes only a single sour note to undermine an effective sermon.

A far more sharply tuned ear is that of Edwina Hunter, teacher of preaching at Union Theological Seminary, who is deeply concerned with how the Gospel can be heard in different cultural settings and shared across cultural boundaries. Her sermon "Holy Ground," preached to seminarians about to embark upon formal ministry, brought Moses' burning bush to life. Citing case after case of heroic action by ordinary Christians in the face of threats and violence, she empowered her hearers to affirm their own sense of vocation to social justice. God's promise of deliverance is resoundingly proclaimed; the presence of God in courageous leadership is joyfully celebrated. Dr. Hunter's hearing of and response to cultural voices makes it possible for those to whom she preaches to hear and respond as well.[3]

Listening to voices in the liturgy

Even for those of us who regularly attend church in an explicitly liturgical setting, it is easy to lose track of the voices that surround the sermon in the worship service. Most liturgical elements are relatively fixed, routine, even rote, in relation to the sermon, and our attention tends to fade when the voices we hear are constant and predictable. Yet the sermon is not the all-important centerpiece of Christian worship, around which all the other liturgical elements cluster.

Whether formal or informal, the rhythm of worship in all of Christian tradition includes praise, penitence, petition, and some form of self-offering in response to God's gracious gift of life in Christ. In all these acts of worship, we function as a community, not merely as an association. In such a context, a sermon that is a dramatic or didactic monologue is clearly out of place, regardless of how entertaining, informative, or inspiring it may be. And the sermon is not simply the climax of the Liturgy of the Word; it is an integral part of the listening and speaking of God and the gathered faithful.

In a liturgical setting there will be other elements as well. Recitation of the creed affirms historic continuity with the church throughout the ages. Collects, litanies, and sung or spoken anthems provide a common grounding for individual expression. Eucharistic bread and wine offer the Real Presence of Christ. All of these features will in turn be set within a yearly seasonal cycle with its related but distinctive themes: the preparation for Christ's coming, the presence of Christ in the Incarnation, the proclamation of the liberating Good News, the purifying vocation of discipleship, the Passion and Resurrection, and the power of God's Spirit poured out at Pentecost. Finally, the same liturgical structure that knits our common life together also provides a place through which we can uphold individuals who are at critical junctures or transitions in their lives—baptism, marriage, ordination, and death.

The interaction of preaching and liturgy, for good or ill, is clear in the celebration and blessing of a marriage. Sometimes there is no preaching at this service; although the names, faces, and fancy clothes may vary from one wedding to another, the couple is simply run through the ritual. On the other hand, given the quality of many wedding sermons, the absence of preaching could be considered a blessing—especially if the sermon goes on about the nature and duties of marriage, when the liturgy articulates this so simply and elegantly. Or if the preacher waxes sentimental about how much everyone loves the couple and wishes them well, when the prayers of the people express it so powerfully. Yet listening attentively to the voice of the marriage liturgy allows the preacher to make the celebration personal. The sermon can clearly, though indirectly, address the unique situation of the couple in light of the Scripture and in the context of the liturgical drama.

Prayers, Scripture, the distinctive shape of eucharistic prayers, the unfolding themes of the different liturgical seasons, pastoral offices, and occasional services are all voices that a careful preacher will not ignore. They are voices that can complement and interact with the sermon. Some so-called liturgical preaching gives awkward recognition to the need for listening to the liturgy by chattering on about liturgical practices, and quoting snatches of phrases from the liturgy as proof texts in the sermon. How much better to see the whole of the worship service as a drama, with the sermon as one of its acts—an act that must be integrated into the movement of the whole drama. In a liturgical setting, the sermon is not the dramatic climax of the worship service!

Listening to the voices within the preacher

Of all the other voices, this is at once the most and least obvious of all. It is the preacher's voice that delivers the sermon, no question about that. But in the attempt to say and hear the word of the Lord, both preacher and parishioner can forget that a *human* voice is the medium of this message. In this respect, the preacher's voice is like all the others I have just discussed. As there is more than one voice in every Scripture text—congregation, cultural context, and liturgy—so there is always more than one voice in the preacher. Preachers can become preoccupied with their own inner voices or pay practically no attention to them whatsoever. If the preacher to whom we listen recognizes and properly uses the distinctive voices within, however, the sermon we hear will be particularly engaging because it will be, as Phillips Brooks described it, "truth mediated through personality." The preacher's inner voices never simply second what Scripture, congregation, culture, or liturgy are saying. Temperament, educational and vocational experience, family history, special interests, secret sins, unresolved resentments, unhealed wounds, fond hopes and faint ambitions—all of these add color to what the preacher says and what the congregation hears.

Some preachers believe that their message gains credibility with the congregation if they let the whole of their own inner experience "hang out." It doesn't. But neither does the message become authoritative if preachers cloak their distinctively personal witness by trying to speak impersonally or *ex cathedra*. The voices within the preacher should not predominate, but neither should they be ignored, suppressed, or silenced in the service of "humility."

I vividly remember a woman who discovered her own preaching voice over the course of two homiletics classes a few years ago. Her roots were Presbyterian, her father a distinguished and erudite black pastor who preached with intellectual precision and emotional restraint. She herself had earned a Ph.D., but left a promising career to respond to a call to the priesthood. Her preaching reflected her family heritage and her personal accomplishments—it was wholly adequate, but not very inspiring.

In other areas of her experience, however, this woman was incapable of *not* being inspiring! Recognizing the gap between her preaching and the rest of her life, she began to experiment with what it might mean to preach with "soul." This was no easy task; it meant swimming against a strong set of currents. But there was a deeper current. As she started listening to certain dimensions of her own experience to which she previously had paid little attention, she began to develop a passionate preaching voice that made the hairs on the backs of our necks stand up. Her preaching was seldom loud, although she had considerable lung capacity; it was not lacking in theological sophistication, for she did not renounce her background or her education. Her preaching never manipulated our emotions, but it was a wonderful orchestration of gift, wound, and vision. Her sermons were utterly unique and transparently selfless in service of the Gospel.

All of us have multifaceted personalities. In attending to many voices, the preacher, in a disciplined, professional way, sits down at the table and enters a conversation with as many of those facets as can be recognized. The sermon resulting from such an investment has the effect of bringing the whole conversation, focused but live, into the midst of the congregation. That is a very different thing for the congregation to hear than a detached report of abstract theological research.

Helping the preacher listen

The preacher has a professional responsibility to attempt to integrate all the voices I have been describing. But no preacher, no matter how professionally skilled, can hear every voice there is to hear, much less hear them in a balanced way. So preachers must rely on the attentive ears of those in the congregation as well as their own.

In listening to some voices, such as those of Scripture or the liturgy, it is likely that the preacher will bring greater attentiveness and insight by virtue of training and experience. But insightful discoveries in all domains of human experience are frequently made by the non-professional. Training in any set of methods can make the user insensitive to some cues, even as it sharpens perception of others.

Preachers must also have help in listening to the congregation. They will have far less to listen to if members of the congregation are not forthcoming about their own experiences. Further, any congregation has experts in certain areas of which the preacher has only a limited understanding. What a pity for a preacher to be denied the unique perspective of a political scientist, an accountant, a poet, a fast food employee, a homemaker, when these are so readily available!

While it may seem presumptuous or intrusive for parishioners to assist preachers' attempts to listen to their own internal voices, the fact is that none of us can hear ourselves fully. We need the help that can only come from honest, caring, perceptive friends and colleagues. Preachers are no exception.

Simply stated, preaching is too big a task for the professional to undertake alone. It is not only imposssible for a preacher to do the whole job; the very nature of the Body of Christ in which the preacher ministers and participates makes it inappropriate. The preaching task begins with engaging many voices in a common conversation.

Endnotes

1 See Ronald J. Allen, *Contemporary Biblical Interpretation for Preaching* (Valley Forge, PA: Judson Press, 1984) for the analysis of this text. The book gives a clear, non-technical account of strategies for listening to a biblical text.

2 Walter Brueggemann, "The Social Nature of the Biblical Text for Preaching" in *Preaching As a Social Act: Theology and Practice*, ed. Arthur Van Seters (Nashville: Abingdon, 1988), p. 158.

3 The full text of this sermon appears in *Preaching As a Social Act*, which includes other sermons keenly sensitive to congregational and cultural voices. See also the sermons of Ronald J. Allen and Don Wardlaw in Don Wardlaw, ed. *Preaching Biblically: Creating Sermons in the Shape of Scripture* (Philadelphia: Westminster, 1983).

4

Discerning a Strategy of Integration

GOOD PREACHING IS INFORMED by broad and deep listening, but it does not simply repeat or even paraphrase what is heard. Listening alone will not provide the focal point. The preacher must also reflect upon the meaning of what has been heard, and chart a clear direction if the word of God is to be heard effectively in a sermon. The sermon is an attempt to integrate all the voices preachers hear and to enter a dialogue with them. Every voice cannot receive equal time—at least not in every sermon—nor will the first or the loudest voice always be the best one to "go with" in shaping a sermon. Preaching cannot be *less* than good listening, but it needs to be *more*.

What is this *more*? Is it a spiritual sixth sense that descends along with the call to preach? Is it conferred at ordination with the laying-on of hands? How comforting it would be to preachers and parishioners alike if that were the case! My father was a minister who preached with great earnestness and care. After one Sunday sermon, a woman came up to my mother all aflutter with enthusiasm. "It is so wonderful to hear your husband preach! When he stands in the pulpit and proclaims the Word, his face positively *glows*. He must live so much closer to the Lord than the rest of us." My mother managed to mumble something inconclusive. She knew that, in the heat of an Alabama summer, and with unusually oily skin, my father's sweat glands had simply been working overtime!

Orchestrating the voices one hears in preparing to preach may ultimately depend upon, and occasionally be graced by, sparks of special inspiration, but by and large the move from attentive listening to responsible speaking involves the exercise of disciplined imagination. The preacher's *attention* must be complemented by *reflection*. Reflection is not rumination or free association. A person who reflects is not simply spinning empty theories, or idly spacing out. We look at ourselves in a mirror as a way of standing outside ourselves; our reflection helps us to see ourselves more clearly, or to see things about ourselves that we otherwise would miss. Similarly, reflective thinking enables us to gain some distance from what we have seen and heard, so that we can put it in perspective. But how does one go about this reflection in sermon preparation?

A fairly straightforward way is for the preacher to ask what kind of sermon the congregation needs to hear—what it needs to learn, how it needs to be invited or challenged to act—and simply design a sermon to match. A gentle jog of your memory will probably shake loose recollections of many sermons, some better, some worse, organized from this point of departure. Do any of the following standard strategies sound familiar?

Personal testimony: "Our text shows us that Jesus changed St. Paul's life. He changed the lives of X and Y; he has changed my life, and he is eager to change yours as well."

Moral exhortation: "Look what happened when Israel disobeyed the Lord, when Ananias and Sapphira lied to the Christian community! Be not deceived, God is not mocked! We will all reap what we sow!"

History/theology lecture: "Today we celebrate the Feast of Anselm, doctor of the church, and formulator of the ontological argument for the existence of God. Anselm was born in ...The ontological argument states that...Anselm and the argument are important to our faith today because...."

Serial study of Scripture selections: "We come now to the ninth chapter of Romans, and Paul's difficult argument concerning the status of the Jewish people. He begins in verse one by saying...."

Evangelistic outreach: "In Jesus' approach to Nicodemus and to the woman at the well, we see a clear picture of how salvation is addressed to each individual at his or her particular point of need."

Systematic treatment of doctrine: "Every year, on the Sunday after Pentecost, our attention is directed by the liturgy and the Scriptures to a fundamental mystery of our faith, which we confess each week without really understanding—that God is Trinity: Father, Son, and Holy Spirit."

Address to an issue of pastoral concern: "Have you ever felt utterly worthless? That you were a walking disaster waiting to detonate? That you couldn't do anything right when it really counted, no matter how hard you tried? Listen to what the writer of today's epistle says: 'The evil that I would not, that I do; the good that I would, that I do not. Wretched man that I am!' I can relate to that, can you?"

Confrontation of a pressing social problem: "In his healing ministry, Jesus touched the blind, the lame, the deaf, the dead, and the leper. Until fairly recently all those stories sounded like so many variations on a single, heart-warming theme. The advent of AIDS has changed things. Victims of AIDS are the lepers of today's society. It sounds wonderful to say that we want to participate in the healing ministry of Jesus, but how many of us have touched—actually touched—a person with AIDS?"

In each case, the result of listening is a clear response to a clearly perceived agenda item. If the listening itself has not been selective, at least the outcome has. And how can it be otherwise? If the preacher simply reports on everything that has been heard in the process of formal and informal sermon preparation, the congregation will probably be swamped with a babble of voices and come away from the sermon with no clear understanding at all. Instead the preacher must step back, think, and then choose a point of reference from which to construct the sermon.

While sermons that address issues having to do with doctrine, history, moral exhortation, or evangelistic outreach need to be preached, there is a danger that, however urgent, such sermons will be insufficiently reflective. Their thrust will be imposed upon, rather than arise from and resonate with, the voices to which the preacher has been listening. These strategies tend to use a pastoral "voice over" to get the message across. Many sermons turn out to be heavy-handed and prescriptive. The preacher's reflections have been superficial; the burden of the sermon is to "improve" its hearers. What is needed is a deeper point of entry for integrating sermon voices that more accurately describes the human condition and evokes a response to the grace of God. I want to suggest such an approach to the shaping of sermons.

Images, narratives, and arguments

Throughout all the varieties of Scripture forms three basic, related, but distinctive motifs can consistently be found. Whether the text is a hymn of praise, a terse teaching, a historical account, a parable, or a theological essay, it communicates by using *images, narratives,* and *arguments.*

The Scriptures engage our senses and our emotions directly by means of images. They also invite us to enter as participants in stories—historical, fictional, and mythical narratives. They further confront us with arguments—orderly presentations of evidence intended to lead us to certain conclusions. In some Scripture texts one or the other of these forms clearly predominates. Psalm 23, Ezekiel 34, and John 10 offer vivid images of God as shepherd, for example. The creation accounts of Genesis, many of Jesus' extended parables, and the gospel reports of his death and resurrection are all presented as narratives, while much of the material contained in the epistles consists primarily of arguments.

There are decided differences between these three genres, yet many biblical passages employ more than one. Jesus' "Bread of Life" discourse in John 6 uses a recurring image in the service of an argument that is set in the context of a story. The images of fire, water, untamed animals, fig trees, grape vines, and olives are all employed by the epistle of James in its argument about the use of the tongue. A brief narration of the Last Supper forms part of the much larger argument concerning divisions in the church that Paul deploys in 1 Corinthians.

Even if images, stories, and arguments do not all explicitly appear in a particular passage, they are part of the broader context of the scriptural conversation. The most poetic expression of thanksgiving or despair arises out of some kind of story, and implicitly makes some kind of claim.

The book of Revelation practically sends us into sensory overload through images that affirm certain claims about the eventual triumph of the risen Christ, so that those whose life stories are threatened can have hope.

The stories Jesus tells in many of his parables are effective in large measure precisely because the images they use are so arresting. The plot line in the Prodigal Son is particularly engaging because the two sons and the father are pictured so boldly. While the telling of such parables is anything but a string of rigorously reasoned propositions, an effective indirect argument is clearly implied.

Theological arguments in the epistles are also liberally illustrated with images and stories. An abstract definition of faith in the eleventh chapter of Hebrews, for example, is immediately fleshed out by a brief retelling of stories about Abel, Enoch, Noah, Abraham and Sarah, Moses, and others. The argument concludes with the breathtaking image in Hebrews 12 of the cloud of witnesses who support us as we run an arduous race.

Images, stories, and arguments are ordinary, everyday modes of communication. There is nothing distinctively sacred about them. Yet it is always through a combination of these that God reveals what God wishes human beings to understand. If preachers want to help us see, hear, taste, touch, smell, understand, and interact with God, their best bet is to take as a point of departure the images, actions, or arguments of Scripture.

Depending, then, upon the thrust of the text and the need of the hour, the preacher will select an image, narrative, or argument as a centering strategy for sermon integration. Sometimes an image, story, or argument in the text will be employed as the primary shaping element in the sermon; at other times the text of Scripture can best be sparked by a parallel or complementary image, story, or argument. While the distinctive shape of every text needs to be understood and honored, sometimes a fresh hearing of a passage rich in images may be helped by an argument. By the same token, a scriptural argument may best be represented as a story or an image.

Images, stories, and arguments, selectively employed, are constant integrating strategies in the preaching and teaching of Jesus. The kingdom of God is not an empire like Caesar's. Picture instead a grain of mustard seed, a buried pearl, a coin that is lost and found. Challenged to debate the legitimate limits of neighborly responsibility, Jesus tells a story about a man who fell among thieves on the road to Jericho. He explains forgiveness with a tale about a young man who demanded his rights, squandered them, came home in desperation, and found himself facing a very different kind of music than he could ever have imagined in his wildest dreams.

Sometimes, instead of resorting to images or stories, Jesus faces down both followers and opponents in blunt, head-on exchanges. "What good is it to gain the whole world, and lose your life in the process?" "You give tithes of the smallest herbs, and neglect the weightier matters of the law!"

To say that sermons are made up of images, stories, and arguments is hardly an earth-shattering announcement, because preachers have always used them. I am not suggesting a new bag of tricks, but expressing my conviction that, in sermons that "work," in sermons that actually make the Good News come alive, one of these three—image, story, or argument—is the orchestrating, integrating principle that shapes the whole sermon. One of the three is chosen as the means best suited for *this* preacher at *this* time with *this* text for *these* people. Images, stories, and arguments serve as sermon-shaping strategies, as vehicles for an experience of the Word that is genuinely sacramental.

To say that sermons need to be strategically shaped in terms of the text's basic message is also nothing new. Frequently, however, this message is regarded as a nugget of spiritual truth that must be mined from the text, isolated, and presented as attractively as possible with the use of illustrations or memorable outlines. Mining and packaging theological nuggets, however, tends to produce flat, superficial preaching—sermons that report what God has done, promise what God will do, and exhort us to let God do it. What we need in preaching, however, is a word that describes and evokes. We need preaching that *is* sacramental, rather than preaching that *just talks* about the sacramental quality of God's self-revelation in history. Sermons that consciously integrate the voices of Scripture, congregation, culture, liturgy, and preacher through a coherent strategy shaped by image, narrative, or argument have an excellent possibility of becoming sacraments of grace to those who hear them.

Each sermon strategy intends a transforming experience of the Good News. The way in which that transformation is prepared, however, differs with each one. The *image* sermon is shaped by the preacher's conviction that a fresh way of seeing and sensing things in the everyday world will generate fresh insight as to how that world is the bearer of God's grace. A *narrative* sermon attempts to engage us as active participants in the sermon's plot; thus drawn in, we will be able to recognize the broken pieces of our own histories as taken up into the powerful healing story of cosmic redemption. An *argument* sermon affirms the fact that sometimes neither images nor stories can deal effectively with missing or misunderstood links in rational understanding, so that explanation rather than illustration is sometimes essential for insight. In each case transformation occurs when grace is mediated through a particular kind of new connection.

To be effective, any sermon can employ only one central strategy. But every sermon needs—whether explicitly or implicitly—to make fresh imagistic associations, assert and support rational claims, and be plotted in effective narrative sequence.

What do these different integrating strategies look like in practice? Let me offer an illustration of each.

Using an image

The image that serves as a "magnet" to bring the various voices together may be one that occurs in the Scripture reading, but it need not be. I shall never forget the sermon preached at my ordination to the priesthood by Chester LaRue, who was responsible for shepherding my family into the Episcopal Church. My ordination took place on St. Joseph's Day, in the chapel of my seminary community.

Fr. LaRue began with a story called "The Eighteenth Camel." An old Arab died and left seventeen camels to his three sons. The terms of his will were explicit. One-half of the camels were to be given to the eldest son, one-third to the middle son, and one-ninth to the youngest son. The sons were greatly perplexed, since seventeen cannot be divided by two, three, or nine. As they were pondering how they might appropriately divide up their inheritance without spilling either their own blood or that of their camels, a neighbor came to their aid. "I will lend you my camel," he said. There were now eighteen camels. The oldest son took one-half (nine camels); the middle son took one-third (six camels); the youngest son took one-ninth (two camels). Nine plus six plus two camels totalled seventeen, and the neighbor took back his eighteenth camel.

From that most unlikely opening, the preacher went on to say that St. Joseph, as depicted in the lessons, was himself an "eighteenth camel"—a non-essential necessity—one who had a critical role to play in a drama of which he was not to be a central character. Seminaries are eighteenth camels, said the preacher; so is the church, and so most especially is the role of the ordained priest. All of these are meant to serve as means to an end; all become idolatrous if they are treated as ends in themselves.

One could hardly imagine a more fitting message for someone soon to take holy orders. It deeply resonated with the lives of others in the seminary community; it addressed the state of the church; it was sensitive to the liturgy of the day.

While I might have nodded wisely upon listening to a sermon that argued the necessity of humility among those in the priesthood, I doubt seriously if the message would have stuck with me. The eighteenth camel, however, is an image that has never receded from the corners of my mind. It calls me back constantly, disarmingly, delightfully, to my role in the family of God.

Using an argument

Dr. Jay Rochelle, dean of the chapel at the Lutheran School of Theology in Chicago, once tackled the difficult passage found in Romans 10, where Paul is trying to make both connections and distinctions between the law of Moses and the law of Christ in the context of discussing Israel's salvation. The passage, in which Paul does some paraphrasing of Deuteronomy 30, is as follows:

> The righteousness that comes from faith says, "Do not say in your heart, 'Who will ascend into heaven?'" (that is, to bring Christ down) "or 'Who will descend into the abyss?'" (that is, to bring Christ up from the dead). But what does it say? "The word is near you, on your lips and in your heart" (that is, the word of faith which we proclaim); because if you confess with

your lips that Jesus is Lord and believe in your heart that God raised him from the dead, you will be saved...The scripture says, "No one who believes in him will be put to shame." For there is no distinction between Jew and Greek; the same Lord is Lord of all and is generous to all who call on him. For, "Everyone who calls on the name of the Lord shall be saved."

Dr. Rochelle then marshalled the following argument, interpreting Paul's interpretation of Deuteronomy:

1) Paul seems to think that the reason why Israel was unable to appropriate God's covenant is that they took for themselves what was available to them only as *gift*.

2) While Gentile Christians may *seem* to have an easier time acknowledging their gifted status in Jesus, Paul knows, and we must acknowledge, that it is no easier for us to receive salvation as a gift than it was for Israel.

3) Many of us try to ascend into heaven or descend into hell to find salvation. Rather than accept the free gift of grace, we are far more inclined to look for righteousness either by pursuing lofty ideals or denigrating the human condition rather than simply taking life *as it is*, which is where Christ meets us with redemption:

> You distance yourself by wishing to slip in between yourself and God some form of religion, be it uplifting your own skill, talent, accomplishment, your ascending into heaven where Christ is, or be it the trashing of yourself, by insisting on a hell of guilt. In both cases we make our demons to be mediators between ourselves and God. We do this at peril to our lives because my demons are insatiable and so are yours. Their appetites are never ending. They imprison us in bondage to ourselves.

4) It is precisely this subterfuge of religion, which knows no denominational boundaries, that Christ comes to destroy:

> So Christ smashes the demons upon the holy rood. In the very moment when it appears that they hold him in sway, God cuts them down in order that he might leap up high carrying treasures in his hand, and you and I are the treasures upraised into new life.

5) Freedom from bondage to self comes from faith in Christ.

> So, if we believe in our hearts that God has raised him from the dead we are, in the very act of faith, recipients of that righteousness and so restored by grace to being who we *are*, not who we fancy ourselves to be, nor whom we accuse ourselves to be. We are recalled and restored to *being* from the depth and the heights of non-being. We are called into the righteousness of our own existence, able to walk forth, freed by grace...You are granted the graceful permission to be who you are and to stop all this nonsense of leaping up into heaven, or of casting yourself down into hell. This is so, even as you hear it.

Notice that, while Rochelle makes effective use of vivid imagery, the driving impetus of this sermon is a tightly reasoned argument. For a difficult passage of Scripture dealing with a difficult truth for us to receive, this sermon may have much more "sticking power" than a sermon that floats an image or spins a story to the effect that "God loves and saves us just the way we are."

This sermon was preached at the final eucharist of a gathering of Lutheran and Episcopal seminarians who were exploring together the theology of ministry. Both individual experiences of call and denominational understandings of vocation were shared. Presumably Rochelle could have used other strategies for this sermon. What was effective in this setting, however, was that although the sermon was thoroughly "theological," it addressed every one of us across the boundaries of our respective theological positions while maintaining the integrity of the preacher's Lutheran perspective. It did not sweep rigorous analysis of issues of law and grace under the table with a dazzling image or a heart-tugging story. The power lay in the argument.

Using a story

I preached the following sermon at the Maundy Thursday liturgy in a parish of which I was priest-in-charge. In this parish there was great reluctance to participate in the foot-washing ceremony. It was also a parish strapped with a large debt service on its physical plant and struggling to get beyond its own survival needs to address the needs of the surrounding community. Since it is quite short, the sermon is presented in full:

"Put your toys back in the toybox!"
"Take your feet off the table!"

Sooner or later kids have to learn
that there are places for things.
And certain places where certain things just don't belong.

Wet bathing suits don't belong on the coffee table.
Chocolate chip cookies don't belong in the middle of your bed.
Goldfish don't belong in the bathtub.

There is a place for everything; and everything has its place.

We also have places for people.
And ways of letting people know when they are out of place.

We put up signs:
KEEP OUT!
NO TRESPASSING!

Some of these signs make sense.
Unless you know how to handle electricity,
you don't belong around high tension wires.
You have no business in an operating room
if you aren't a medical professional.

But there are other kinds of signs.

As a boy, growing up in Alabama,
I saw signs over restrooms and water fountains:
COLORED
WHITE
I saw signs in buses that sent dozens of black people
into four rows of seats at the very back,
while eight or ten white passengers
had the rest of the bus all to themselves.

A place for everyone, and everyone in their place.

Sometimes the place markers don't even have to be printed up
and posted.
You can read KEEP OUT in people's faces.
You can hear NO TRESPASSING in their tones of voice.
Sooner or later you will get the message.
All you have to do is pay attention.

Jesus didn't pay nearly enough attention to social boundaries.
He didn't fit in where he was supposed to.
And he kept on turning up where he didn't belong.

He partied with tax collectors
that everybody knew were traitors.
But he threw respectable businessmen out of the temple
when they were merely trying to make a living,
and doing it by providing a necessary service.

He read the riot act to priests and theologians,
but he spoke words of forgiving kindness to street people.

Tonight he is really out of place.

The one whom the disciples call "Master"
   strips down in front of them,
   and dons the garments of a slave.
No self-respecting Jewish male would dream
of stooping to that.

Foot-washing?
   That's a job you give your Gentile.
   Or, if you can't afford to keep a Gentile,
   you pawn it off on one of the women in the house.

Can you believe it?
Jesus doing slaves' work,
   women's work,
   the work of a racial alien.

The very same hands—
washing feet one minute,
   breaking bread the next.

It's disorienting.
It's socially disruptive.
It's downright disgusting.

Look here!
My dirt is my dirt. Your dirt is yours.
I don't want to deal with your dirt.
And I don't want you to deal with mine.

"NO, LORD. YOU SHALL NEVER WASH MY FEET!"

But Jesus, well, he's kind of stubborn.
He just can't take NO for an answer.

Dear friends in Christ, neither can we.

Here images are used, and an argument is implied, but what integrates this sermon is the story of Jesus washing the disciples' feet at the Last Supper. The strategy is to set up a contemporary situation, and then to draw the listeners into the cultural circumstances that surround the gospel account, with the hope that the similarities will resonate without being "tagged" as such. Then the listeners are brought directly into the story through an identification with Peter. Finally those who hear are invited to discover a sense of solidarity first with Peter and then with Jesus, which should help them recognize their need both to be washed and to wash, in spite of comfortable but artificial social norms.

It should be evident by this point that the integrating story need not be a biblical narrative. Many times a fresh connection with the Gospel can be more effectively achieved with stories from non-biblical sources that embody the thrust of the Good News in unusual or unexpected ways.

A distinctive voice

The basic sermon strategy at work in each of these three examples is different, but the ultimate intent is the same—an accurate description of both grace and the human condition that evokes a response to the Gospel. While the fundamental strategy in each sermon is clear and distinct—image, argument, or narrative—each also makes use of the other two strategies in supplementary ways. While some people are temperamentally disposed more to one strategy than another, most of us have different needs at different times in our lives. Even if we have a clearly established comfort zone, we need to be challenged on occasion to see how the workings of grace look and sound through other eyes and ears. We need this challenge so that we do not create God in our own image, and unconsciously relegate others to the status of second class citizens in the kingdom. Such stretching is essential to our developing maturity as members of the Body of Christ.

As they learn the art of preaching, it is essential for preachers to discern their own distinctive preaching voice. It is almost always the case that, by virtue of temperament, training, previous experience, and other factors, individual preachers will be more comfortable preaching primarily from one point of departure. Some folks just can't tell stories; others can't use images to save their souls. Still others can hardly follow an argument, let alone construct one. All preachers begin with the gifts that have been given them, and then branch out to meet the needs of other persons and situations.

That branching out is as important for preachers as it is for members of the parish congregation—for the same reasons and for others as well. The need for preachers to be able to address different kinds of people "where they are" is obvious; furthermore, some situations clearly seem to call for one strategy rather than another. There is a limit to what stories and images can do for theological understanding on Trinity Sunday. Arguments about the Incarnation seldom accomplish much on Christmas Eve, just as doctrinal analyses of the Atonement achieve little during Holy Week.

Preaching at particular pastoral offices needs to be similarly sensitive. It is conceivable that a wedding or a funeral could be the occasion for an argument sermon, but frankly, the possibility seems highly remote to me. Again, arguments may be more difficult for the very young or the very old to follow, but a steady stream of story sermons may alienate parishioners in a university chapel.

A sermon style may also be chosen to fit a particular liturgical rite. Either an image or an argument may be more appropriate than a narrative on Ash Wednesday, depending on whether the emphasis is "getting in touch" with our mortality through the image of ashes, or encouraging a healthy perspective on

Lenten discipline, such as the one clearly stated in the bidding prayer that invites the congregation "to the observance of a Holy Lent."

The basic strategy chosen will by no means write the sermon. What it can do is to help the preacher make vivid connections between Scripture and our experience that will evoke our response. This is far more effective than a strategy exhorting us to fulfill abstract obligations.

The task of preaching, however, involves more than listening and integrating; it also involves plotting. That will be the focus of the next chapter.

5

Plotting a Journey of Surprising Recognition

HEN MY DAUGHTER KRISTEN was about two years old, our family went on a weekend camping trip. We stayed at the most domestic of all possible family campgrounds, complete with every amenity and protection, and we could not have been more safe and secure—or so we thought. As we were sitting at the picnic table in the gathering twilight, seemingly from out of nowhere a loud buzzing insect zoomed in. It did not attack or sting Kristen, it simply "buzzed" her—darting without warning across her field of vision a few inches from her face. She was understandably startled, then terrified, and it took us several minutes to calm her down. She did not stay calm, however. Her innocence with respect to the great outdoors had been shattered. Kristen was sharp enough to perceive that if one bug can dive bomb you once, any number of other bugs can get you anytime they want to. It was a long weekend as we dealt with

constant alarms evoked by anything that flew anywhere within my daughter's field of vision.

Nor did we leave the fear at the campground when we returned home. There was no longer any safe place for Kristen. (And precious little peace and quiet for the rest of us!) She started and screamed and wilted and wailed at the slightest indication of a flying insect of any sort—including harmless flies. I am sure that some of what she shrank from were sheer figments of her tortured imagination. We tried every trick we could think of to settle her down and disarm her fears. We comforted, we cajoled, we distracted her attention, we made jokes with her, and occasionally we told her to straighten up and behave herself. All to no avail. Rather than receding, the problem seemed to compound.

Debbie, one of my wife's sisters, was living with us for the summer and taking a course my wife was teaching called "Literature for Children." The final assignment in the course was to write a children's story. Debbie was drawn to the family predicament in which we were all embroiled, and wrote a story about a little girl who was afraid of bugs.

One day the little girl wanted to go out and play on the swing. She was afraid, because she knew there might be bugs waiting for her, but she wanted to swing so badly that eventually she just had to go outside. Sure enough, she spied a bug and screamed at the top of her lungs. As the scream died away into silence, the girl heard a strange, tiny noise. It was the bug, giggling at the horrendous fuss that he had been able to get the girl to make over him—such a small harmless creature! Suddenly it seemed funny to the little girl as well. She joined in the laughter with the bug that had scared her, and (the story concluded) "turned a somersault in the grass."

After she finished writing it, Debbie asked Kristen if she would like to hear a new story. "Yes!" came the expected response. Kristen listened with rapt attention. At the end of the story, she said intently: "Read it again." The story was reread many times during the next few days. No words were spoken by anyone about bugs or the fear of them, but by the end of the week the problem had simply vanished.

More was going on in that story reading, obviously, than entertainment. A healing was taking place.

The stories that punctuate sermons now and then are often regarded as more interesting than the points which those stories are intended to illustrate. (Indeed, it is often the case that people remember the story and retain no memory at all of what the story was trying to get across.) But the fundamental importance of stories lies not in their interesting details or their illustrative value. It does not lie in the stories themselves, but in how hearers can be drawn into them. If a point of identification can be established with characters who are engaged in realistic interaction, there is a possibility that such an identification can have the effect of reshaping the life-stories of those who hear the story in the sermon.

The carefree, safe world of my small daughter was shattered by an alien intruder. Reassurances to the effect that "the bugs won't get you" were seen for what they were—potential lies at worst, and impossible promises at best. Exhortations and moral edicts were of no avail; Kristen was simply incapable of the behavior they urged and demanded. Healing came through her participation in the story. The healing story Kristen heard did not deny the threat she had experienced, but it set the threat in a context that transformed it. A broken narrative of actual experience was taken up into a richer, more rounded and open-ended narrative of possible experience.

The sharing of such a narrative, of course, is precisely what Gospel proclamation is all about. The life, death, and resurrection of Jesus, as the focal point and culmination of God's dramatic interaction with humankind, is offered to us. Not as a denial of our fear, wounds, ugliness, and death, or as an escape from it "in the sweet by-and-by," but as an invitation to bring the shattered bits of our broken personal and corporate histories into the transforming drama of God's salvation history. So there is a profound theological reason for seeing story as narrative or as a clue to what is perhaps the most important reflective reference point from which to shape sermons that are to be genuine performative utterances.

But there is another reason why a narrative sense seems to be critical in the shaping of sermons. Books we read can be read again. Well-organized essays give the eye and the mind fixed points of reference; they provide a map to chart the terrain of the exposition or the argument. Paintings and photographs can be seen all at once. While we may spend a great deal of time taking in the details of what is before us, we always have the whole scene as a basis for reorientation. Sermons, however, are addressed to the ear over a period of time—perhaps fifteen minutes, perhaps longer. We cannot hear a sermon all at once the way we can see a picture. We cannot stop the flow of the sermon and return to a place where we got off track, the way we can if we lose the thread of an argument that appears in print.

Listening alone is not effective for some kinds of learning. Try describing a complex line drawing, a detailed abstract painting, or even the scene in a childhood memory to a group of people who know nothing about it. Or try explaining in a single hearing, without being interrupted by questions, a complicated argument that has taken you several readings to grasp, but now seems to make good sense. It doesn't work very well, does it? That is because both speaking and hearing occur in time, and one-way oral transmissions are not efficient ways of communicating complex diagrams, visual fields, or sophisticated concepts. "Let me show it to you," we finally say in frustration, or "You would have to have been there," or "Why don't you read the argument for yourself, and then we can talk about it."

We seldom have the same difficulty with a well-told story, however. There is a chrono-logic at work, an unfolding pattern that enables us to hold a significant number of complex details in place, and also that whets our appetite and sharpens our anticipation for what the storyteller will tell us next.

In a word, a story offers what neither argument nor image can present by itself: a plot. Plots are schemes of organization that are "ear-friendly"; they have the potential for drawing us in as we find points of identification with the characters and circumstances of the story. The Maundy Thursday sermon in the last chapter does not lecture us about our responsibilities as Christians regardless of our social inhibitions, but attempts to invite the congregation into the tension of the story as Jesus insists on washing Peter's feet.

Sermons may be well organized, the way an essay or a legal brief is organized, but careful construction may not prevent the mind from wandering, if there is not an orienting plot through which the listener can enter in and follow along. By no means should all sermons be shaped by stories, but all need to be *plot-ted* in order to engage us and address our quest for meaning. They need to bring us along on an unfolding journey. They need to show us pictures, present us with arguments, or share stories with us—in a purposeful, narrative, dramatic process.

We need to be taken, like Joseph, into bondage in Egypt, and clearly shown that, in spite of our ignorance or denial, we

are in a situation of bondage. We need to join with the children of Israel in the drama of deliverance, not just to have the
highlights of the Exodus summarized for us in three parallel
points. A thickening of the plot, a dramatic turn of events, and
a sense of future possibilities are integral to a short story, novel,
movie, or TV drama, and are just as crucial to the sermon.

A sermon should move through carefully developed se-
quences, rather than stand on a series of static principles, even
if the sermon is integrated around images or arguments. Stories
by themselves will not automatically produce a good sermon.
The plot of the sermon will be identical to the plot of a story
only on those rare occasions when the sermon actually consists
of only one story. The plot line of the whole sermon is critical,
regardless of the basic strategy of integration chosen, or the particular way that strategy is employed. It is not only possible but
often easy to unfold a series of images or to deploy the steps of
an argument in an engagingly plotted sequence.

A surprising recognition

In each type of sermon, effective plotting holds the attention
of the congregation and heightens its sense of anticipation. The
point, however, is not simply to hold an audience spellbound.
If sermons do their work well, they will lead their hearers
through a process of personal discovery. This will not be a discovery of something that is totally new or utterly foreign to their
previous experience, however. The discovery will be a fresh realization of a truth that has been vaguely felt, long forgotten, as-
sented to but not much thought about, often considered but
always dismissed as "too good to be true." Good preaching
brings, as Fred Craddock says, "a shock of recognition."[1]

When we truly experience the Gospel, it is a revelation to
which we say "Yes! Of course! I see it now! It didn't seem obvi-

ous, but it makes sense! If this is really true, then I don't have to go on living the way I have been!" The good news of Jesus Christ fulfills our deepest hopes. Its transforming power does not turn us, as with a magic wand, into utterly different creatures; rather, it re-creates, resurrects, and restores. It shows us how our lives and our histories are encompassed by grace. Repentance and conversion mean that we can, at different points in our experience, find new meaning in "the old, old story." The effect need not necessarily be earth-shattering (indeed, substantive conversions are often more subtle), but good preaching always takes us on a journey that leads to surprising recognition.

How, then, do the sermons we looked at in the previous chapter develop a plot that leads us on such a journey? Only the Maundy Thursday sermon is explicitly shaped by a story, but each sermon has a narrative structure operating at a level that is deeper than the image, argument, or story in and of itself.

The recurring images of the "eighteenth camel," for example, are not presented in random order. After the bemusing mathematical conundrum focusing our attention on the camel that resolved the inheritance dispute, the preacher moves us quickly to St. Joseph, then to seminaries, next to the church, and then to the ordinand. As I remember, the sermon concluded with the picture of still one more "eighteenth camel"—Jesus, who gave himself as a mediator in bringing us to wholeness with ourselves, with each other, and with God.

To begin the sermon by saying, "You know, Jesus is a camel of sorts," would have been attention-getting, to say the least. But it probably would have gotten the preacher lynched (or at least turned off by his audience). Furthermore, the association of the image of "camel" and the concept of "ministry"—unforgettable precisely because it is so unusual—could not have been established had not the different dimensions of that association been deployed according to a carefully constructed chrono-logic. The sermon does its work primarily by images, but the images are carefully shaped by the plot. We know, of course, that Jesus is the priest from whom all priesthood derives its meaning and that Jesus "emptied himself" on our behalf. We also know that we ought to "be like Jesus," regardless of whether the form of our priesthood is lay or ordained. And yet, to be led to see that Jesus is a camel of sorts—after the groundwork has been carefully laid for this startling image—is to be taken on a journey of surprising recognition. We realize in fresh and empowering ways what Jesus has accomplished for us, and what he has given us the power to do for others.

In the argument sermon about law and grace, it would have been easy enough to remind the congregation that Paul argues justification by faith throughout the Letter to the Romans, and to tell the congregation what Paul tells the Romans. Easy enough, and homiletically soporific. So instead of merely repeating Paul's argument, Dr. Rochelle re-creates it. Armed with an imaginative insight born of careful exegetical research, he takes Paul's paraphrase of Deuteronomic phrases—which are all but Greek to the average ear—and snaps them dramatically into a culture driven by a hopeless and perverse quest for self-esteem. As Paul does with Deuteronomy, Rochelle does with Paul. Each takes a theological concept and turns it simultaneously upside down and rightside up—rescuing it from demonic and enslaving forms of "religion," so that it can point the way toward covenant companionship with God.

Notice how each step of the argument clearly moves ahead but remains closely linked with the step before it, while preparing the hearer for the step that is to come. The listener is not told what to think, or handed the results of a theological analysis, but is invited to walk along with the stages of the argument and experience directly the liberating power of its conclusion. The effect is one of participating in conceptual detective work. As we approach the end of the sermon, we do not find ourselves thinking: "Yes, I really do need to work on my self-esteem," or "I'm OK, you're OK," or "I see that I must try to have the faith that Jesus loves and saves me in spite of my selfish self-assertion and self-denial." Instead, we experience freedom from the damnation of desperate doing, as we recognize with surprise what we knew all along: that Jesus' death and resurrection are God's way of sweeping us into the arms of divine acceptance.

The Maundy Thursday sermon is obviously shaped by more explicitly narrative considerations. We are, by sermon's end, taken directly into the many simultaneous levels of dramatic tension at work among Jesus and the disciples in the upper room. But notice how the narrative structure of the whole sermon is not simply a re-presentation of Jesus' foot washing and his direct confrontation of Peter, for the events surrounding the Last Supper are taken into the much broader narrative of the sermon. For the sermon to be effective, it cannot simply tell again the story of the upper room, and then add a few concluding comments such as, "We should let Jesus (in the person of each other) wash our feet—even as the liturgy invites us to do now—and we should depart from this place ready to wash the feet of others, just as Jesus has washed ours." Ho hum. Yes, of course. There would not be enough energy generated by this strategy to evoke any kind of surprising or transforming recognition.

If, however, our ambiguous experience of social boundaries—some legitimate and some harmful—is vividly called to mind, we experience a tension similar to that which may be at work in Peter's conflicted feelings. Peter's story becomes our story. Then the actions of Jesus can enter our story, as they did Peter's, to heal and transform us at a point of deep resistance. If this happens, then we may experience the washing of feet in the Maundy Thursday liturgy as a release from sinful and self-constricting social barriers. We will find that, to our surprise, the Jesus we thought we knew has met us in a way that we could not have expected. When this happens, preaching nourishes, sustains, energizes, and brings us back with a healthy appetite for more.[2]

When sermons don't work

In light of what we have been suggesting in the last two chapters, a few words might be in order as to why even the most earnestly prepared sermons sometimes don't fly. In describing such sermons, parishioners offer one of two complaints: either that they "couldn't figure out where the preacher was going," or that they could figure out *exactly* where the preacher was going!

If listeners lose track, it is usually for one of two reasons. In some cases, the sermon is little more than a series of free associations from the mind of the preacher. These may come from personal experience, or they may be a "grab bag" of scholarly but obscure observations. Since there is either no plot to the sermon or no integrating strategy for all the voices, the plot of the sermon zigs and zags like the trail of a jackrabbit. Lots of words and thoughts and pretty pictures about love or forgiveness, or a series of wandering remarks about the readings—but no clear sense of direction. It is no wonder in such cases that the listener gets frustrated and shuts down.

On the other hand, listeners may lose track even though the sermon is very tightly organized. If its organizational pattern is just a dull outline of topics, complete with sub-points, each duly illustrated, the ear will simply be unable to follow what the eye, with repeated readings of a printed text, might comprehend well enough. In neither case has the sermon been written to be *heard*. In neither case is there any recognition that the sermon is a dramatic art form, not a collage of ideas or a research paper.

Sometimes sermons, unfortunately, are entirely too trackable. The listener knows, almost from the first minute, precisely where the sermon is going to end up and how it is going to get there. It then becomes sheer agony to endure the blow-by-blow, inch-by-inch account of the simplistic plot you know inside-out and backwards. The problem here, of course, is that the reflective imagination of the preacher has not been sufficiently sensitive to the creative freshness of grace. If there is no surprising recognition, no fresh awareness of how we are confronted and converted by the power of God's love, the sermon will be as nourishing as leftover oatmeal, served up yet again in the same tired old way. Who could have any appetite for that?

Sermon-shaping and conversion

In this chapter and the one before it I have been discussing my belief that good sermons are creative actions—performative utterances—more than historical or theological reports, and that they accomplish their intended work by evoking recognition rather than by urging and exhorting. Images, stories, arguments, and narrative structures are effective sermon strategies because they provide ways for describing creation, sin, grace, and redemption, rather than merely issuing strings of prescriptions, obligations, and imperatives. If, after unfolding a sermon shaped by image, story, or argument, there is still an urge to tell the congregation "the moral of this story (or image or argument) is," then either the sermon itself is not sufficiently well-shaped, or the preacher has a problem with personal anxiety or with understanding how God's authority most effectively operates in preaching. In any case, there is a serious misunderstanding both of preaching and of the Good News. Good sermons will not need to assault hearers with how they ought to accept the grace they cannot earn.

Much of the anxiety and misunderstanding that leads to heavy-handed preaching comes from the fact that preachers and listeners may not be able to trust the process of revelation through which, God promises, the word proclaimed will not return void. Transformation takes time. Conversion does not happen all at once. Even sudden shifts in our spiritual understanding and action have been in preparation under the surface for some time, and will take some time to become fully assimilated into our lives. No one sermon does its work instantaneously, and spiritual growth never hangs on the "success" of a single sermon. The biblical text from which we preach is itself the result of an extended process—a process in which we are called to participate and to trust.

But what are we talking about when we speak of conversion or transformation? Sermons often urge us to undergo it; people frequently give testimony as to how God has "changed" their lives. It is very easy for such sermons and testimonies to convey the impression that what we expect from or have experienced in a conversion is simply a change in circumstances—the "bad" parts surgically removed and replaced with "good" parts—the surface of our lives supernaturally rearranged. In this understanding of conversion, it is as though the plane of our natural existence could be reconfigured by asking God to make a guerilla raid: to come in and expand or contract its boundaries.

But genuine conversion is an awakening to the realization that we are grounded in a third dimension: the grace of God. In conversion we come to see that what we had previously perceived as a "flatland" has all the time been upheld, permeated, encompassed, and transcended by the love of God. The flat circle on which we live turns out, we discover, to be a very limited dimension in an all-surrounding sphere.[3] "Surely God was in this place, and we did not know it!" Thus enlightened, we are freed to engage the world with new energy, hope, and direction.

Preaching takes the features of everyday existence—images, stories, and arguments—and plots them into a journey that brings us to a recognition of divine depth that changes both nothing and everything. Good preaching helps us to this kind of conversion, a realization that Christ came *in* human flesh to *redeem* human flesh, not to haul us out of it. Conversion is ultimately the work of God's Spirit. The tasks involved in shaping a sermon simply focus the possibility of that transformation.

Having reflected at length about the underlying elements in good preaching, we are now in a position to address some more practical concerns:

1) How can this understanding of preaching help you as you listen to the sermons that are preached in your parish every week?

2) How can you help your parish if it is in the process of looking for a new pastor or priest who will be able to preach effectively?

3) How can you sustain the preacher you have, or the preacher you plan to call, in his or her preaching ministry?

4) How can you express your understanding of preaching in the sermons that may already be sounding within you, or surely

will begin to well up inside if you seriously reflect upon the preaching process.

We now turn to each of these issues in the third part of the book.

Endnotes

1 Fred Craddock, *Preaching*, (Nashville: Abingdon Press, 1985), p. 160.

2 The importance of narrative quality in sermons has been described clearly and thoroughly by Eugene Lowry in a number of books and articles. Much of what I say in this chapter is a development of insights he offers. The interested reader may wish to spend some time with any of the following: *The Homiletical Plot: The Sermon as Narrative Art Form* (1980); *Doing Time in the Pulpit: The Relation Between Narrative and Preaching* (1985); *How to Preach a Parable: Designs for Narrative Sermons* (1989); "The Narrative Quality of Experience as a Bridge to Preaching" in Wayne Bradley Robinson, ed., *Journeys Toward Narrative Preaching*, (1990).

None of these are technically forbidding for the lay reader, and *The Homiletical Plot* would be an excellent next step for those who are interested in exploring preaching further.

A very different kind of book, but one that simply and succinctly presents all the dimensions of preaching is O. C. Edwards' *Elements of Homiletic: A Method for Preparing to Preach* (1982).

3 This image is an elaboration of Edwin Abbott's *Flatland: A Romance of Many Dimensions* (1952), a fascinating fantasy that presents a two-dimensional world of triangles, squares, pentagons, hexagons, etc., locked in a deadly struggle for status. The more sides a figure has, the higher its social status, and the more it oppresses fewer-sided figures. One day a sphere passes through the plane of Flatland, revealing to the citizens the restricted dimen-

sions of their world, the limits of their perspective, and the tragic stupidity of their social struggle. Most of the citizens of Flatland pass the revelation off as a hallucination ("A crazy dream of an expanding and contracting circle!"). One lowly square, however, gets the message. By listening to the words of the sphere, which are at first unintelligible, he eventually comes to see what it means to be in a three-dimensional world.

Celebrating Your Distinctive Preaching Ministry

6

Listening to Preaching

EVERY TIME A SERMON is preached, an evaluation is going on. It may be fair or unfair, sophisticated or simple, carefully considered or spontaneous, fully conscious or only vaguely so. Based on the ideas I've suggested thus far, it should be possible to propose a set of criteria you can employ to assess the quality of sermons you hear. It is surely a better thing for us to evaluate sermons with clear standards of judgment than it is for us either to be swept along by a preacher's enticing but empty rhetoric, or to impose demands on a sermon that are little more than personal axes clamoring to get reground.

But you and I do not come to church for the purpose of listening with arms folded and minds calculating, so that, at sermon's end, we can hold up flash cards and compare them with those put up by other parishioners: "I'd say it was an 8.7!" "Nah, I wouldn't give it a bit more than 7.2!" We come to church not as food critics for the local newspaper, but as hungry people who need to be nourished for growth and service.

Indeed, our knowledge of that need sometimes inhibits our attempts at deliberate evaluation.

Yet backing away from it only sends the process underground. Paradoxically, failure to evaluate sermons effectively keeps us from hearing them well. And the other side of the paradox is equally true: lack of careful hearing keeps us from effective evaluation.

Properly understood, evaluation of sermons is not a matter of "thumbs up" or "thumbs down." Rather, it is a matter of listening with discernment to how God may be addressing us with the life-giving word—regardless of how polished the preacher or substantive the sermon. God's word can survive both good and bad preaching (sometimes, in fact, it may face more of a challenge with the former than the latter). The hearer's task is to listen intently for the Word that comes through the preacher's words.

Frankly, this is easier said than done. When a small group of seminary preachers convenes in my homiletics classes, I always tell them in the feedback offered after the delivery of an in-class sermon that I want them to tell the preacher and each other *what they heard* of the word of God through what has just been preached. Almost without fail, the discussion sessions at the outset of the course run something like this: "I really liked the way you said..." or "I disagree with your interpretation of..." or "It seems to me that your message might have been more effective if you had...." I do not think this failure to follow instructions results from an inability or an unwillingness to do what is asked. Nor does it arise, I am convinced, from the effects of a formal theological education. It comes from the fact that sermon hearers, like preachers, often listen *prescriptively* rather than *descriptively*. In other words, we listen for what we like or dislike, agree or disagree with. The end result, of course, is that we do not pay attention to what is actually being said, and we are likely to miss a significant dimension of what is there to hear. Any evaluation that follows from such distracted listening is tenuous at best.

If, in listening to preaching, however, I can be alert to the meanings that a sermon is both shaping and making space for, I will probably also be able to say how I have been helped to hear the message by the way the sermon has been prepared, and the way in which it has been delivered. I will also be able to imagine how the message might have been presented more effectively than it was. Sermon evaluation is not a demand for the sermon I would rather have heard. That sermon may or may not need to be preached. The issue is, how did this sermon do its own particular work, and how might it have done so more effectively?

Yet simply to be told to "listen carefully to what the preacher says" is not enough for most of us to go on. We need help in learning what to listen for. The preceding chapters have not attempted to offer a check list by which you can weigh your preacher's sermons in the balance and find them "Excellent/Good/Fair/Poor" or "Credit/No Credit." Instead, they have proposed a simple but fairly substantial set of questions to ask of a sermon, a set of suggestions as to what to listen for in preaching.

Questions for evaluating sermons

Put succinctly, in any sermon we need to be listening for all of the following:

1) What *voices*—in Scripture, culture, congregation, liturgy, and the preacher—has the sermon invited and enabled us to hear?

2) What is the integrating strategy in the sermon? Has it focused our listening to the word of God primarily through an image, a story, or an argument? How have the various voices we have heard been brought together in clearly directed conversation?

3) How is the sermon strategy *plotted* to help us recognize God's grace at work in us and in the world?

To ask these questions is to search for the dynamic pattern of the Gospel at work in the center of the sermon. And that pattern will be there, regardless of whether or not the preacher has consciously woven the sermon with these questions in mind. Perhaps the pattern is vividly, breathtakingly present; perhaps the pattern is evident mainly through its absence. No matter. Reflecting on the sermon with these questions in mind, you will either see with more clarity where the sermon did go (and thus experience its power all the more), or you will get a sense of the sermon that was trying to come to life, and be nourished to some extent by that awareness.

The same basic questions can be framed another way:

1) How does this sermon manifest the preacher's ability to listen?

2) How does this sermon speak for and with the Christian community, even though it is being delivered by a single individual?

3) How does this sermon show us God and the world, rather than simply tell us what what we ought to do or be?

4) How does this sermon call forth an awareness of God's already-present grace, rather than merely exhort us to catch up with it?

5) How does this sermon encourage the ongoing process of God's redeeming work in the hearts and lives of hearers?

6) How does this sermon function as a performative utterance? To what extent is it an extension of the enfleshed and saving Word, rather than simply a report of what happened "once upon a time"?

7) If the sermon does not seem to do much of any of these, how is it trying to do so, or how might it do so?

It is possible to become more sophisticated in your analysis, of course. Not in the detached mode of a food and wine critic, but with the excitement of one who appreciates nourishment all the more by virtue of understanding both nutritional needs and culinary arts. How, for instance, do the dimensions of image, narrative, argument—as drawn from Scripture and in coversation with culture, congregation, liturgy, and the preacher's own personality—interact? What voices, if any, are being given freest expression over the course of several weeks or months of preaching? What are the strengths of that? Are there voices, particularly voices that are difficult or uncomfortable for us to hear, that are being soft-peddled or ignored? How might you invite such voices into the sermon process as it continues to unfold?

It goes without saying that the reflective process I am describing here should not go on solely within the confines of your own head. If you are living in a household with others—family, friends, those who share the rent in your apartment—they need to be invited into the conversation as well. They may have a slant that would never occur to you. (It helps, of course, if they have heard the sermon; but, surprisingly, it is not absolutely necessary. You can bring them up to speed by a quick summary of content and reflections.) Sermon dialogue of the type we are describing is, bluntly put, crucial to the life of a parish community. The fact that it seldom transpires is all the more evidence of how much it is needed. How helpful it might be, to you and your preacher, if, at least on occasion, you requested the opportunity of continuing the dialogue!

"Pre-listening"

All I have said so far is about the process of listening to, reflecting on, and talking about the sermon itself. There is, however, another important responsibility of the sermon listener: to engage in the discipline of "pre-listening." More and more parishes and denominations are following a lectionary that prescribes Scripture lessons for each Sunday of the year. Often in churches where a lectionary is not used, the preacher will decide well in advance of the preaching date the Scripture to be used on a given Sunday. Failing that, a healthy hassling of the preacher early in the week will yield the necessary information (as well as send a salutary and significant signal). The bottom line is that we need to gather for worship with a general awareness of where our attention will be directed. Each lesson should be read, preferably more than once, during the preceding week.

But not just read. With respect to each reading, ask and note down, preferably in writing:

1) What are the primary images which these Scriptures depict? How do the Scriptures appeal directly to the senses of the hearing community?

2) What actions are going on in the texts? Who is doing what, for or to whom? How do these actions pick up from verses prior to the reading? How are the actions picked up in verses that follow it?

3) What messages are being delivered? What concepts are explained? What complex issues are struggled with?

4) How do the readings carry forward or contrast with ideas that have been the subject of lessons in previous weeks?

(If you have time, ask the same question in looking ahead to forthcoming readings.)

5) What echoes do you hear of issues and questions that are alive in your parish, in the news, in your own personal experience?

6) What hard questions, ambiguities, infuriating pronouncements do the texts present—the sorts of things that make you say: "I'll bet the preacher won't touch that with a ten-foot pole, but I sure would like to hear *someone* take that on in a sermon someday!"

Additional questions for a sermon discussion are provided at the end of the book.

If you come to worship "primed" with this preparation; if you ask God to address your hunger in light of these "pre-listened" lessons, the chances are excellent that, even if the preaching seems impoverished, you and God will prepare a nourishing meal anyway. And it just might be the case that the preacher will do a better job—not just in your hearing, but in the hearing of all those gathered—if you and others make that kind of preparation. For preaching, after all, is not a monologue, but a community conversation.

If both we and the preacher are as well prepared in our own respective ways as time will allow, what we can expect to experience together is a fresh hearing of "the old, old story." Having been told many times over to "taste and see that the Lord is good," through the interactive process of speaking and hearing we will "taste [the Lord] again for the first time." This will not consist simply in receiving new information, although new information may help us to hear. It will not be simply a heart-warming emotional titillation. It will be a confrontation with the Gospel that calls us toward, and empowers us for, continual conversion, the result of which will be further participation in God's kingdom of peaceful justice.

7

Finding a Good Preacher

HEN PARISH CHURCHES ARE faced with the task of calling a new priest or pastor, "effective preacher" is usually very high on the list of desired qualifications. The increasing demand (or at least the longing) for good preaching is a documentable phenomenon. It suggests that a deepening hunger is beginning to prevail over listless loss of appetite, and this is a trend worth celebrating. In the long run, if more and more congregations are up front about their expectations and act upon their longings, the church may experience a revitalization that will never come from simply bringing in business administrators, program directors, and personal counselors, individually or in combination. The skilled exercise of these other functions is important, and is no less a ministry than preaching. But all of these tasks can be handled by other professionals, by competent and committed laypersons, and even to some degree by an ordained minister—so long as that minister sees his or her primary calling to be one of a creative, sacramental extension of the Word.

The early church faced a critical administrative problem over equitable distribution of food for the needy. Failure to address this problem immediately and decisively might well have spelled the demise of the Christian community. After all, feeding those in dire need was an essential element in the ministry of Christ. Had stomachs gone empty, and spirits been outraged by negligence or favoritism, the word proclaimed would have been as dead as faith without works. Yet, faced with the situation, the apostles are reported to have said: "It is not right that we should neglect the word of God in order to wait on tables." This was no snobbish assertion of clerical privilege. It was, rather, a recognition of where their particular focus should center. Other persons, just as competent and devout, should be appointed for this particular ministry of justice and compassion, the apostles said, "while we, for our part, will devote ourselves to prayer and to serving the word." The writer of Acts goes on to say: "What they said pleased the whole community," and "The word of God continued to spread" (Acts 6:1-7).

I know of a large church that exercises an exceedingly ambitious ministry in a complex urban environment. The place is constantly alive with activity. The overall administrative demands are overwhelming. One of the priests, at a particular point of crunch, moved to take over more of this load. He was told kindly, but in no uncertain terms by one of the laywomen, herself up to her eyeballs in responsibilities: "We can do this. We need you to pray for us and to preach to us. If you preach and pray faithfully, we will find the resources to do what God has called us to do. If you get distracted from that, this whole enterprise will be in jeopardy."

The search process and preaching

We need our ordained ministers to be effective preachers, perhaps above anything else. That is easy enough to say. The question is, how does a parish go about securing a good preacher? It is surely fair to say that this can only happen if those who are charged with the search process for filling a pastoral vacancy are not only desirous of and sensitive to good preaching, but also competent to select a pastor or priest who will fulfill this critical function.

Having said that, it must be admitted that there is no sure-fire way of making a "right" choice. It is ironic that in the most significant of life's decisions—choosing a vocation, choosing a spouse, buying a home, deciding on a college, changing jobs—there is no way to do such an exhaustive investigation that "picking a winner" can be guaranteed. We invest great care and energy in these watershed decisions, obviously, but the dimensions, complexities, and variables always outrun the time and talent we have for investigating them. So it is with the calling of a new minister. You don't ever really know what you are getting, in any of these choices, until the decision is made and you begin living with the consequences of the best choice you were able to make at the time.

It does not follow, however, that any of these choices might as well be made by flipping a coin. With respect to a search for a good preacher, there are questions to ask, things for which to look, factors to consider.

Hear them preach

It would seem to go without saying that, if you are on a search committee, you need to hear prospective candidates preach. But it needs to be said, because the exposure that new congregations and search committees get to the preaching competence of pastoral candidates is often next to none. There are some practical reasons for this. No search committee can or should visit a prospective candidate's present parish over an extended period. Yet a single "trial sermon," wherever it is preached, is woefully inadequate and unfair to all concerned. The preacher may be having an unusually bad day (or an unusually good day!). It is important, therefore, in assessing the quality of a serious candidate's preaching, to do all of the following: obtain (directly from the candidate) copies of several manuscripts, audio tapes, and video tapes (if available) that let you hear the patterns of preaching. Insofar as it is possible, everyone participating in the search should read/hear/watch all the sermons available. These should be discussed among committee members, using points of reference such as those referred to in the last chapter.

It is also important to talk with other persons about the prospective pastor's preaching ministry. It is, in all probability, inappropriate to talk with members of a candidate's current congregation. But, after requesting and receiving assurances of professional confidentiality, it is possible to talk with preaching peers of the candidate—those in the same city, the same diocese, those who attended the same seminary. (Not only is it appropriate to ask the candidate for the names of such persons, it communicates to the candidate in a healthy way how seriously you take the preaching ministry.) Do not, incidentally, forget to talk with the candidate's bishop or judicatory supervisor, and with the professor of homiletics with whom the candidate studied preaching.

Discuss preaching

There are a number of questions to be posed to candidates directly. How widely do they read (and by no means just in theology)? How (in some detail) do they prepare for preaching—for individual sermons, for seasonal preaching, and for the long haul? What kind of continuing education experiences in preaching—formal and informal—have they taken advantage of? How consciously do they attempt to vary their preaching style according to the shape of the Scriptures and the contours of congregation, culture, liturgy, and internal voices? How intentional are they in bringing before the congregation voices of the unfamiliar, the marginalized, those whose voices are ignored or denied? Are they sensitive to the complexity of gender and minority issues? How do they orchestrate the convicting and the comforting dimensions of the Gospel?

What role do their congregations have in preparing sermons? Do interested persons meet with the preacher to help in the preparation and to reflect on the presentation? How does each candidate interact with other preachers? ("I just don't have enough time for that," is a significant piece of information.) What systematic ways do these preachers have for personal, ongoing evaluation of their sermons? How clear are the candidates about their particular gifts and limitations, and their unique preaching "voices"? How do the preachers attempt to capitalize on perceived strengths and compensate for weaknesses?

The personality of the preacher

There are other matters that the search committee needs to address on its own. What distinctive personality does each candidate for the pulpit seem to have? How will that appropriately challenge and nurture particular individuals in your parish, and the distinctive parish personality as well? In what respects is the potential newcomer a carbon copy or an antithesis of the most recent preacher who has occupied the parish pulpit? Are you aware of tendencies to look for a clone, or to combat a previous style? In what respects do those tendencies seem to be healthy or unhealthy?

Admittedly, this list of topics for investigation is both long and thick. It does not need to be followed legalistically, but it should alert you to how complex are the factors that go into the person of a preacher and the ministry of preaching. Looking over the list, you might be inclined to conclude that nobody could possibly be good enough! But these are not so much achievements to tote up as they are growth points to reflect upon in talking to the one who may soon become your preacher. Freshness, imagination, and interest in growth are much more important than years of service, accolades, polish, and formal credentials. What both you and the candidate are attempting to discern is the degree of mutual "fit," rather than whether either preacher or parish is "good enough" for the other.

A personal observation may have some relevance. Having taught preaching for several years in three seminaries and a variety of workshop settings, I have found that there is no direct correlation between how old people are when they begin to study preaching, and how effective they are likely to become. Young persons tend to be in some respects more venturesome and agile; older persons bring a wisdom and seasoning to the preaching process that can only come from getting knocked around by life. The strengths of each can be marshalled effectively to compensate for the limitations, and each can learn from the other. It does not follow automatically that a highly educated person is a better preacher than someone with a more modest educational background. Even those with limited educational training can learn rapidly, granted a basic intelligence and desire. Formal education can provide rich resources for preaching, but well-schooled individuals can be as dogmatic as unschooled persons can be open-minded.

It is a great tragedy, however, when a candidate for a pulpit is dismissed out of hand as being "too intellectual." A pontificator of abstractions is one thing, but high intelligence, like artistic genius, can speak to all types and conditions of humankind. What a pity if distinctive gifts are summarily dismissed!

Having said what I have about the relative insignificance of age as a factor in learning how to preach, I have to say on the other hand that age makes much more difference if the preacher has been preaching for some time. A thirty-year-old who has been "doing it" for five years and has settled into a comfortable pattern may not be nearly as effective a preacher as one who is sixty, just out of seminary, and fired with energy and imagination. The point to be made here is that, just as there is more to preaching than appears on the surface, so there is more to the preacher than a superficial assessment can disclose.

It cannot be emphasized too strongly that, just as it would be profoundly self-defeating to listen to sermons with a rating sheet in hand, so it would not prove helpful to submit your candidates to an interview or a background investigation that is not so much "thorough" as it is a kind of power play. Humility in search of humility; hunger in search of hunger; a mutual delight in savoring and celebrating the nourishing word of God, both as it is prepared and as it is served: that is what all participants in the search process are attempting to manifest and discern.

Of course, there are qualities in a preaching candidate—positive and negative—that forever elude any categorization, no matter how exhaustive. Even if there were time to track down substantive data on all these questions (and any number of others besides), there is a sense in which the task cannot be "finished." Yet you can trust that, if you do your work conscientiously, your committee will, through prayer and the leading of the Spirit, know the right preacher to call when the right time comes—however long it takes. This is not a cop-out, but a recognition that the factors you weigh are never merely a balance sheet of quantifiable positives and negatives.

You are looking for a priest/pastor who is a good preacher; but part of what makes for a good preacher is a sense of preaching as itself a pastoral ministry, a priestly vocation. The pastor is a shepherd—one who leads by living alongside, one who eats, works, plays, laughs, and cries with those in the community. The pastor tends, cares for, and (when necessary) lays life on the line for the sheep. The priest is a mediator, a bearer, one who gathers the offerings of joy, pain, confusion, grief, anger, failure, and insight and, by setting them apart for a holy use, imbues them with sacramental significance. One can recognize pastoral priestly qualities in a preacher, even point to specific ways in which they manifest themselves, though never definitively or exhaustively. When, with the poet, I have counted all the ways "I love thee," have I really pinned down the essence of love? Preaching, when all is said and done, is a love affair.

Yet, let us not wax sentimental. Theologically we know that ultimately there is one Good Shepherd; there is one Priest; there is one who has embodied the proclamation of the Good News. All pastoring, priesting, and preaching participates in and flows from the ministry of Christ. The search committee in which you participate is looking for a human instrument. It will not demand deity in its preacher; it will not idolize its preacher. It can, however, trust that the priestly, pastoral touch of the Word made flesh will operate in and through the preacher who is keenly conscious of being an "eighteenth camel."

8

Helping Your Preacher
Toward Deeper Listening

T HE CALL HAS BEEN issued, and the candidate has accepted. Your responsibilities for securing an effective pulpit ministry are finished. Wrong! They are only beginning. No matter how gifted the person you have called may happen to be, the quality of the preaching you hear will be significantly affected by the quality of ongoing support your preacher receives. Regardless of how good your preacher is, he or she can and should continue to grow. You have not only a stake, but a critical role in your preacher's development. There is not a preacher alive whose ministry of proclamation will not be seriously eroded if it is not shored up by intentional engagement on the part of the congregation.

The same principle applies to the preacher who has been in place for some time. If anything, the urgency here is greater. In many parishes there is vague or vigorous discontent with preaching that is, in fact, quite poor. The tragedy is that, to some extent, the complaining parishioners bear a considerable responsibility for the condition with which they are unhappy. There is no preacher beyond all hope of remediation, but help must begin in the congregation. While outside resources may be important as well, they will be effective only to the extent they are integrated within a network of energetic commitment on the part of the folks at home. Only a preacher who is utterly arrogant or uncontrollably anxious is incapable of improvement. And even then, there is always hope that these spells may be broken.

Time for preparation

What can you do to help your preacher preach? To begin, you can recognize that preaching takes time. Words that heal, nurture, and challenge do not just roll off the preacher's lips spontaneously. The more natural or easy preaching sounds, the more effort it takes, week in and week out, to sustain the enterprise. There is all the difference in the world between Gospel proclamation that is graceful and that which is glib; graceful preaching is a gritty business.

We know all this at a certain level, yet it is a knowledge that often does not get translated practically. Precisely because the responsibilities of parish ministry are so many and varied, it is very easy for the ordained minister's time to be "nickled and dimed" away. No task in itself seems to make an inordinate demand, or to take excessive time. "Pastor, while you are out already, could you please just..." and suddenly the morning, the day, the week has all but disappeared. Your pastor or priest must take ultimate responsibility for protecting sermon preparation time, as well as for prioritizing the full range of pastoral duties and employing time efficiently. But understanding and support from the congregation is essential. Some sermon preparation can be done in bits and snatches here and there, but uninterrupted blocks of time are needed as well. And the preparation for any particular sermon is almost never effectively done in a single extended sitting.

Odd though it may sound, some of the most efficient preparation for preaching is that which is not done specifically for the next pulpit appearance, or even for any particular sermon. In his book *Between Two Worlds: The Art of Preaching in the Twentieth Century,* John Stott counsels preachers to build in time for general study—an hour each day, a morning each week, a day each month, and a week each year. This is work time for the preacher, not something to be saved up for a day off, for the yearly vacation, or even for a spiritual retreat. Even though they may seem to come from out of the blue, the fresh associations, illuminating connections, and creative insights which make for preaching that transforms actually emerge from a deep well of resources that must constantly be replenished. When the only time spent in sermon preparation is explicitly task oriented, the well sooner or later runs dry. Then the preacher strains harder and harder to pump less and less. Long hours of labor may be spent grinding out tedious and lifeless results—while other legitimate, even urgent pastoral needs are ignored. Or the increasingly frustrated preacher may escape into the trivial pursuit of non-essential pastoralia, rationalizing that there are, after all, "more important" things to do than spend time in the study trying to cook up another unappetizing sermon. (At this point the canned homily service we met in the first chapter is only a toll-free telephone call away.)

It is important, then, not only to allow your preacher space for sermon preparation, but also actively to protect such space, to encourage others to do so, and to build study time into your minister's job description.

Dialogue

It is also critically important for a preacher to be in constant contact with the congregation about the ministry of the word. "Nice sermon" doesn't cut it, nor does behind-the-back grousing. More and other is needed than straightforward agreement or disagreement (even if reasons are attached, and the package is delivered with suitable cordiality). What is most helpful to preacher and congregation alike is ongoing and substantive conversation about preaching. Sermon feedback that is really a consumer reaction to a purveyed commodity is inappropriate if the word of God is truly alive and active.

Some preachers may initially be threatened when you say: "I'd really like to find some time to talk with you about the implications of your sermon." But if, with individuals and groups, formally and informally, such interaction becomes habitual, both preacher and parishioners alike can only grow. Sometimes there will be particular points of interest or even healthy contention arising out of a sermon. Perhaps the discussions will spill over into scriptural, theological, cultural, or personal concerns. When this occurs, a sermon's effectiveness goes beyond questions of how well it was researched, argued, illustrated, or delivered. Instead, it becomes a catalyst for further theological reflection for everyone, and a jumping-off point for further homiletical development on the part of the preacher.

For this process to be most effective, however, it should not take place only after the fact. As suggested earlier, you can be incorporated into the process of sermon *preparation* as well as encouraged to participate in sermon evaluation. A time can be set aside, well in advance of the preaching date, for you to come together with the preacher. Having previously read the lessons with care, everyone may profit from a focused, brief presentation by the preacher of salient information derived from the exegesis of Scripture. You may be invited to reflect upon biblical insights in light of where the congregation and the culture are, of upcoming liturgies, and of what has been preached in preceding weeks.

We are not talking here about a sermon constructed by committee. We are instead imagining the exciting possibilities of calling together a community of proclamation. With such support the preacher will be able to hear more broadly and deeply as she prepares; you will have more of a stake in what is proclaimed. You will gain more from the sermon as it is preached for having worked with the preacher. Progressively more sensitized to the dynamics of the preaching process and to the energies that shape effective preaching, you will enter more fully into the preaching event. In short, all participants will come to realize in progressively greater depth how the word is active, powerful, alive, and gracefully transforming.

Since it is important that the preacher's private study focus on more than a single sermon, sermon preparation/evaluation groups should also participate in long-range, seasonal planning. They can meet at stated points (say, quarterly) to reflect upon the direction sermons have been taking in the last several weeks, again, in the context of pastoral and cultural concerns.

To preach with, for, and to you effectively, the preacher needs to get to know you more deeply. As you become better acquainted, share your hopes and hurts, your nagging questions and stimulating insights. The preacher is not an expert in your area of personal and vocational experience; whether you are a nuclear physicist, nurse, real estate agent, homemaker, or librarian, you bring a distinctive window on the world and on the word of God. If the insights derived from such a vantage point are not made available, your preacher, your parish, and the whole Christian community will be denied a perspective only you can offer.

Beyond the parish

There are resources outside the parish community which your preacher should be encouraged to explore. Pastors and priests seldom have financial resources in abundance. Basic necessities for self and family have an obvious priority. So can you imagine what a check designated for additions to your preacher's library might mean? It will be a gift that graces at many levels simultaneously.

How much does your parish budget set aside for clergy continuing education? Probably not enough. Why not push for a budget line item for (or gather a group of contributions toward) sending your priest or pastor to a preaching workshop or seminar, such as those offered by the College of Preachers in Washington, D.C.? Your preacher can also be encouraged to spend time with other preachers talking about the craft of preaching in general as well as about particular ideas for specific sermons. Out of such interactions may come regular pulpit exchanges, which can be invigorating for preachers and parishes alike. (If nothing else, both may discover how good they have it by comparison!) Such interchange is an aid to collegiality and goes a long way toward preventing professional loneliness.

Ministering to the preacher

If you have a preacher who may not have had the benefit of good training in homiletics, or who may be experiencing "homiletical burnout," it is, of course, important to proceed with compassion and sensitivity. Your preacher is a human being, who may well feel somewhat inadequate already. It goes without saying that the opening line of a conversation on preaching is not: "Last Sunday's sermon was lousy!" or even "I have some problems with your preaching." Begin instead with a genuine comment on whatever has been preached: there will always be something that can serve as an authentic point of engagement. God has promised that the divine word will not return empty—in spite of, if not because of, the preacher. The church believes that the sacraments are valid regardless of the moral worth of the minister. This does not mean that tales told by idiots are, by divine transmutation, rendered the songs of angels. But the Word will go forth—one way or another—even if it only creates a deeper hunger for better nourishment.

Begin, then, with that word, wherever you can find it, even if the preacher seems, in your opinion, to have botched it completely. Talk with the preacher about the importance of the ideas the sermon has attempted to address. Draw him into dialogue, not about the sermon, but about where the sermon seems to be trying to go. The result may surprise you—instead of defensiveness, you may encounter a gratitude that practically overwhelms you. Your preacher may well be starved for some kind of collegiality, and every bit as hungry as you are for a substantive taste of the Word.

If all else fails, two recourses remain, neither of which should be undertaken in isolation from the other. You may need, at last, to confront the preacher, gently but firmly, privately or with the support of duly constituted lay leadership. Preaching is, after all, a primary pastoral responsibility. An intervention of sorts, leading to clarified expectations and accountability, may be appropriate. Perhaps such a confrontation may even lead to changes in other pastoral responsibilities in order to make more time for preaching.

The second thing you can do is redouble your own efforts to discover what God seems to be saying in the texts upon which your priest is preaching. They may provide some ideas for approaching the conflict redemptively. Such an effort will at least address the lack you are experiencing, and you will not be found before God as one who demands of someone else what you are not prepared to do yourself.

Last, and most important, for good and poor preachers alike, prayers and intercessions should constantly be made. There is no more demanding task in ministry than preaching. Your preacher wrestles not only with homiletical techniques, personal strengths and weaknesses, rigorous exegetical requirements, a host of administrative hassles and value conflicts, and only God knows what else—but also wrestles with "principalities and powers" in standing to proclaim the Good News. There are all kinds of forces—religious and secular—with a vested interest in keeping us all in bondage to the rulers of "this present darkness." Prayer for and with the preacher is not an effort to get God to "fill in the gaps." It is a conscious upholding of human efforts so that they may be touched by grace, and transfigured into a power for cleansing, nourishing, and re-energizing. Preaching and praying, in other words, are ultimately inseparable.

9

Voicing the Sermons that Come from Within

B Y THIS POINT IT is probably apparent that, as a layperson, you have a critical role in the ministry of preaching. If preaching is what we have been describing it to be, it is not for professional preachers only. It is not just that preaching is too important to be left up to them alone, although that is true enough, but that preaching, broadly and rightly understood, is a mutual ministry. It really cannot be done without lay participation. The only question is how intentionally and effectively those on both sides of the pulpit undertake the full scope of their particular responsibilities, and uphold the work of those on the other side. The proclamation of the Gospel is the task of the church. You are a minister of the church. You have a ministry in preaching.

It may also be that your ministry *in* preaching includes a ministry *of* preaching. This is not to say that God is calling you to pursue ordination. In an age of professionalization, it is not surprising that when many people feel within themselves the stirring of a call to Christian ministry they assume they are being called to wear a clerical collar. I recently saw a cartoon in which three priests are addressing a single parishioner who is standing alone in the middle of a row of church pews. "You mustn't go to seminary," they tell him. "There won't be anyone left for us to minister to!"

My concern here has nothing to do with whether or not you have a vocation to ordained ministry, but with how you will exercise your preaching vocation as a layperson. If, in fact, you discipline and develop your sermon listening skills, if you take an active role in the support of preaching in your parish, sooner or later you are going to find bits and pieces of sermon ideas percolating in your head, and probably even whole sermons welling up inside you. Sometimes these sermons will, in some respects, be better than what you regularly hear. You cannot tune and train your own particular preaching ear without discovering that you also have a distinctive preaching voice—a voice that yearns for expression and that God's people (both inside and outside the church) need to hear. What should you do about that?

Your first reaction may well be an immediate "I could never preach!" Apart from the predictable anxiety surrounding the undertaking of any new enterprise, there is surely a deeper hesitation: "I do not have the authority to speak God's word. That only comes with the call to, preparation for, and official recognition of ordination." Such a feeling is understandable, but it may not be entirely accurate.

Not long ago I was participating with a small group of seminarians in a preaching-listening class. A woman had just finished delivering her sermon, and, after sitting quietly with her sermon for a few moments, we began to talk about what she had said and how it had affected us. Several participants noted that the woman had spoken effectively and powerfully from the Letter to the Hebrews as to how God is fully present with us in the midst of suffering and evil. She admitted that the message of the text had gripped her strongly, but she also confessed how terrified she was in presenting it. Pressed as to the source of her anxiety, she responded, "It's a question of authority. Do I really have the authority to announce the Good News? It isn't difficult for me to stand up and tell people what they ought to think or do. But to announce what God has done for them in Jesus—that is something else! You really have to know how you stand with God in order to do that. You can't preach what you haven't experienced."

That led us into an extended and fascinating discussion that went far beyond the scope of the sermon and its delivery. We realized that authority in preaching was a much more mysterious thing than the credentials, the charism, or the chutzpah to "tell people where to get off." Anybody can order other folks around; it is another thing entirely to stride into Egypt, Babylon, or Nineveh (or even the parish pulpit) and announce God's deliverance. The protests and excuses come thick and fast: we are insufficiently experienced, we are "only a youth" (in spiritual maturity, if not in age); we are not eloquent, but slow of speech; we are people of unclean lips, we dwell among a people of unclean lips who will not believe or listen to what we say. We are paralyzed until we hear God's "I will be with you" in the depths of our experience. When we do hear that reassurance, however, we also know that to hear is to be liberated for faithful obedience. When we speak out of such obedience, those who hear us will recognize what listeners perceived in the preaching of Jesus: a speaking with authority.

The woman who preached the "authoritative" sermon on the high priestly presence of Christ in the midst of our suffering was not ordained. And the fact that she was preparing for ordination had nothing to do with the authority of her preaching. The reticence you may feel in expressing the sermons that will begin to bubble up within you is healthy—but it has to do with waiting for God, rather than with fearing that "fools rush in where angels fear to tread."

By no means am I suggesting that you and your preacher will be arm wrestling for the pulpit. We are talking instead about a process of discovering how appropriately to celebrate a collegial ministry. How, then, might your preaching ministry manifest itself?

Lay preaching

To begin with, it is not necessary or even possible for you to deliver all of your "own" sermon material. A significant part of your own ministry of preaching will occur as your ideas find a voice, orchestrated with those of others, in the sermons your preacher will offer. When it comes down to it, who "gets the credit" (or bears the burden) is not important, because we are members one of another. Ministry is not a matter of star players and solo performances. There can be deep satisfaction in experiencing how the word of God that you hear takes different forms through the preaching of others.

But there may be times and places when the word to the faith community will best come through your own hands and face and vocal cords. By this I don't mean simply giving a pitch for a balanced budget on "Stewardship Sunday." If you are actively participating in the kind of preaching process described in the last chapter, there may well come times when your ordained minister, along with others in the preaching group, will recognize it is your voice that needs to articulate what has been emerging out of this group. This will be particularly true if the fundamental image, narrative, argument, or plot of an emerging sermon has come as an inspiration through you. (By far the most effective sermons are those which are distinctively colored by the particular vision of an individual preacher—and no other preacher can deliver that sermon with the same voice as its primary author.) When this happens, your minister and the others in your preaching preparation group will offer you the same support of prayer and practical suggestion as you have regularly offered to them. It will be a risky business, of course. You will do well to take off your shoes in front of the burning bush. But the bottom line in such a hair-raising venture will be an experience of "Surely I will be with you."

The formal Sunday worship celebration is not the only place where lay preaching can occur. There are other occasions in the life of the church when the word of the Lord can be spoken as effectively, if not more effectively, by a lay minister. (The power of the Cursillo movement, when healthily manifested, is a solid witness to this truth—although it is by no means the only one.) Should you have the opportunity to engage in such a preaching mission, the principles of preaching briefly sketched in this book will help you frame and shape your sermon. And you should by all means consult your pastor or priest as you feel the need—either for general suggestions or to discuss particular issues of exegesis, form, or delivery. You have been a source of help and inspiration for your preacher; grant him the same privilege.

If your parish minister has seemed unable or unwilling to preach effectively for some time, it may be that your best means of surviving the sermon is to listen, on a regular basis, for the sermons you need to hear instead. In the long run, I believe, that is a more salutary strategy than heading off to church each Sunday with the day's newspaper surreptitiously tucked under your arm. Even if your preacher is consistently excellent, you may discover that you benefit even more by shaping a sermon of your own that parallels or complements the one that is delivered aloud to the whole assembly.

Students in my preaching classes often have an initial resistance to giving sermons in class. "This is not 'real preaching,'" the students say, "if they are not done in the context of the liturgy." There is a measure of truth in that. As the students and I work together, however, we discover something surprising. As we listen to members of the class preach very different sermons (sometimes on the same text) we come to realize that similar sermonizing is actually going on under the surface all the time at the Sunday liturgy. While only the parish priest is speaking the sermon aloud, all sorts of sermons are dancing about in the minds of the listeners—from sullen protests or barely squelched "Amen's," to vigorous debates and creative sermons that go off in altogether different directions. Part of your ministry in preaching may consist in expressing such sermons yourself—prior to, during, or subsequent to the service—and encouraging others in the congregation to shape and share their own.

Preaching outside the church

There is still another dimension of the preaching ministry that is not only appropriate to lay ministers, but is their particular province: the proclamation of the Gospel outside the confines of the established church. Even to suggest this option is to raise all the ambivalent and unpleasant associations that go along with street corner preaching and intrusive, button-hole evangelism. But do your best to set those associations aside for the moment, and allow yourself instead to enter a different setting.

There is a burning sun and a dusty road, and a man trudging along wondering what in the world a person like him is doing in a place like this. His name is Philip, and what he is *not* is a professional preacher. He knows that, and the whole church knows that. He is, in fact, one of those people who has been singled out and set apart by the church to oversee that important work of fair distribution of food to those who are needy and have no status in the eyes of the world. He has been appointed to this task precisely so that the apostles will be free to devote themselves to "the serving of the word."

Philip is on the road not because he has been given a clear mission, but because he has felt a definite but unspecified nudge. Then the monotony is interrupted by a distant rumble—the chariot wheels of some dignitary who is just passing through. As the chariot approaches, however, Philip notices that the passenger does not seem to be standing (or sitting) on his dignity. Obviously a foreigner, he is reading from a scroll containing the words of Isaiah.

"Do you understand what you are reading?" Philip asks.

"I really could use some help," replies the foreigner.

This response comes from someone who has everything and nothing. He enjoys power, wealth, prestige, and high political position, but he is set apart because of his race and because he is a eunuch. He is reading about a mysterious figure who himself seems to have been isolated and set apart. The pain and possibility in this identification with the Suffering Servant is all but unbearable. "In his humiliation justice was denied him. Who can describe his generation?"

"Will you tell me, please, who is the prophet talking about?" he asks. And starting with the Scriptures, Acts 8 tells us, Philip begins to preach the Good News about Jesus.

Philip's opportunity was not an isolated event, nor did it come up simply because no apostles were ready to hand. Philip had just come from a preaching mission in Samaria. After the Ethiopian eunuch was baptized, Philip found himself whisked away for another preaching mission in Azotus; he then engaged in itinerant preaching from there to Caesarea.

And Philip wasn't the only one. The response of the early church to the first wave of persecution, Acts tells us, is that those who were scattered abroad "went from place to place proclaiming the word." This persecution puts us soberly in mind of another preaching mission by another non-apostle that did not end nearly so happily. The preaching of Stephen got him killed—but it also served as a catalyst for the preaching of Paul.

Perhaps we tar and feather a certain kind of evangelism because we shrink from the pain and possibility of preaching itself in its most fundamental form—the announcement of Good News to the poor, release of the captives, recovery of sight to the blind. That news is not received with open arms by all.

And yet, what God said to Moses, Jesus repeats to the disciples: "I am with you—regardless."

When all is said and done, there is a sigificant sense in which none of us will be able to survive the sermon. At least not the way we are. The graceful Good News engages us in a continual journey of dying and rising. I have talked throughout about preaching as a creative, transforming, performing word—a word alive and active, a word that does things, a word that gathers our broken histories up into the dramatic action of cosmic redemption. Old things pass away (often painfully) at the creative word of the one who says: "Behold, I am making all things new."

As a lay minister you share in the ministry of proclamation. One of the notions to which you (as well as your ordained sisters and brothers) may need to die is the notion that you are meant by God to be only a passive recipient of the word of preaching. But there is a new life on the other side of that dying for all the ministers of the church. Welcome it. Pick it up. Celebrate it.

10

Suggestions for Sermon
Discussion Groups

G ATHERING IN SMALL GROUPS to reflect upon the week's sermon (or any sermon that has recently been heard) is an excellent way to enhance the value of preaching in your parish and to grow as members of a faith community.

Part One: Objectives

When you meet for such a discussion, it is important to remember that the principles of good preaching described in this book are also relevant to your discussions about the sermons themselves. Therefore, certain intentions will shape the comments, questions, and evaluations shared among the members of an effective sermon reflection group.

1) The goal of your discussions is to facilitate an even deeper hearing of the sermon, not simply to report the feedback of each member of the group.

2) You will seek to have a genuine and open-ended conversation about the meaning of the sermon, rather than a series of opinions or "position statements" by individuals in the group.

3) Your observations about the sermon under discussion will be more *descriptive* than *prescriptive*.

4) Instead of insisting upon your own particular insights and interpretations of the sermon, you will try to evoke and draw out the insights and ideas of every member of the group.

5) You will see the interactions of the group as a continuation of the preaching process that has already been focused for you by the sermon.

6) The primary objective of your sermon discussion will be a mutual opening to further transforming action by God's Spirit, not a debate, a tug-of-war, or an exchange of ideas for their own sake.

Part Two: Questions for Evaluation

With these six objectives in place, the sermon reflection group may find it helpful to address the following sets of questions as developed in chapter 6 of this book.

1) What *voices*—in Scripture, culture, congregation, liturgy, and in the preacher—has the sermon invited and enabled us to hear?

2) What is the integrating strategy in the sermon? Has the sermon focused our listening to the word of God primarily through an image, a story, or an argument? How have the

various voices we heard been brought together in a clearly directed conversation?

3) How has the sermon strategy been *plotted* to help us recognize God's grace at work in us and in the world?

These same basic questions can be framed another way:

1) What do the words of the sermon tell us about the preacher's ability to listen?

2) How does the sermon speak for and with the Christian community, even though it is being delivered by a single individual?

3) How does this sermon show us God and the world, rather than simply telling us what we ought to do or be?

4) How does this sermon call forth an awareness of God's already-present grace, rather than merely exhort us to catch up with it?

5) How does this sermon encourage the ongoing process of God's redeeming work in the hearts and lives of its hearers?

6) How does this sermon function as "performative utterance"? To what extent is it an extension of the enfleshed and saving Word, rather than simply a report of what happened "once upon a time"?

7) If the sermon did not seem to accomplish any of these, how did it try to do so?

Part Three: Further Questions for Evaluation

Additionally, you may find some of the following questions helpful as catalysts for reflection and insight.

1) How did this sermon connect to:
   —the liturgy of the day?
   —events that have been in the news this week?
   —ongoing issues of concern in the culture?
   —joys, problems, and sorrows of those in the parish community?
   —your own raw edges?
   —other sermons that have been preached in previous weeks?
   —the ministry of your church in the world?

2) To what images, arguments, and narratives in Scripture did the sermon draw your attention? How did the sermon try to focus that attention?

3) Describe in as much detail as possible the "plot" of the sermon? Into what kind of journey did it invite you? What were the different stages of that sermon journey?

4) Where did the sermon leave you? How are you thinking, feeling, and acting as a result of listening to the sermon? In what direction does the sermon invite you to go next?

5) Are there ways in which the sermon left you feeling
   —confused?
   —angry?
   —grateful?
   —empty?
   —nourished?
   —questioning?

—in significant disagreement?

—confirmed and centered?

—eager to talk about it?

—alienated?

—connected to others?

Describe your experience in relationship to *specific parts* of the sermon.

6) How have members of the goup from different backgrounds and with different life experiences heard the sermon? What have these perspectives contributed to differing understandings of the sermon? How would this sermon strike those

—older than you?

—younger than you?

—of the opposite sex?

—of a different race or ethnic group?

—of different economic circumstances?

—of different education?

7) To what extent did the sermon pull you beyond a preoccupation with your immediate desires, fears, and needs to those of people with whom you have little in common, or who frighten or threaten you?

8) What did the sermon tell you about the distinctive personality, experience, and concerns of the preacher?

9) If you had been preaching on this text, how would you have approached it differently?

10) What did the sermon tell you about the people and the conditions of the biblical setting from which the Scripture lessons were drawn?

11) How was your understanding of the history of the church, or of Christian doctrine, enriched, contradicted, or challenged by the sermon?

12) How did the sermon ground you more fully in God's love?

Part Four: Wrap-Up

If the members of your group are not able to respond to some of these questions, try to identify what the reasons for this might be.

If, as a community of sermon hearers, you can clearly sense difficulties in the sermon, what other listening, integrating, or plotting strategies or skills would help in the sermon's proclamation of the Gospel? Try to be as specific as possible.

Finally, what might you be able do to assist your preacher? How might you supplement on your own what the sermon offers?

OWLEY PUBLICATIONS is a ministry of the Society of St. John the Evangelist, a religious community for men in the Episcopal Church. Emerging from the Society's tradition of prayer, theological reflection, and diversity of mission, the press is centered in the rich heritage of the Anglican Communion.

Cowley Publications seeks to provide books, audio cassettes, and other resources for the ongoing theological exploration and spiritual development of the Episcopal Church and others in the body of Christ. To this end, it is dedicated to developing a new generation of theological writers, encouraging them to produce timely, creative, and stimulating publications of excellence, and making these publications available widely, reaching both clergy and lay persons.